Careers in Focus

Careers in Focus

WRITING

THIRD EDITION

Ferguson
An imprint of Infobase Publishing

Careers in Focus: Writing, Third Edition

Copyright © 2007 by Infobase Publishing

All rights reserved. No part of this book may be reproduced or utilized in any form or by any means, electronic or mechanical, including photocopying, recording, or by any information storage or retrieval systems, without permission in writing from the publisher. For information contact

Ferguson
An imprint of Infobase Publishing
132 West 31st Street
New York NY 10001

Library of Congress Cataloging-in-Publication Data

Careers in focus. Writing.—3rd ed.
   p. cm.
   Includes index.
   ISBN-13: 978-0-8160-6596-7
   ISBN-10: 0-8160-6596-9
   1. Authorship—Vocational guidance—Juvenile literature. 2. Editing—Vocational guidance—Juvenile literature. I. J.G. Ferguson Publishing Company. II. Title: Writing.
   PN153.C38 2007
   808'.02023—dc22

Ferguson books are available at special discounts when purchased in bulk quantities for businesses, associations, institutions, or sales promotions. Please call our Special Sales Department in New York at (212) 967-8800 or (800) 322-8755.

You can find Ferguson on the World Wide Web at http://www.fergpubco.com

Text design by David Strelecky
Cover design by Salvatore Luongo

Printed in the United States of America

MP MSRF 10 9 8 7 6 5 4 3 2 1

This book is printed on acid-free paper.

Table of Contents

Introduction

Career opportunities for writers can be found not only in publishing, but also in film, television, radio, advertising, business and industry, science and medicine, and the arts. And writers are no longer limited to traditional print media—books, magazines, and newspapers. They write for all kinds of media, including the Internet and other electronic multimedia. Kinds of writing vary from painstakingly technical to wildly creative, from factual to fantastic.

Writers are often behind-the-scenes workers. Most writing careers involve concept development, research, interviewing, collaborating with other workers, as well as the actual crafting of words to be written, spoken, or sung. All writing careers require a love of words and a talent for manipulating language. A few of those careers are presented in this book. Included are jobs in advertising, public relations, music, sports, publishing (books, magazines, and newspapers), radio and television, film, science, and business.

Education requirements for writing jobs vary from a high school diploma to advanced degrees in both writing and an additional specialty. For example, a science writer might be expected to have a degree in biology as well as a journalism degree. Although college-level courses in writing, English, or journalism are highly recommended for most writing positions, many writers start from another career and find they have an ability and liking for writing. A computer software designer might discover on the job that he or she is good at writing computer manuals, or a fund-raiser might find that he or she has a special talent for composing grants

Salaries for writing careers vary as much as the types of jobs available. A poet may earn only a byline on a published work while a best-selling novelist may earn millions in fees and royalties. Most writers who work full-time jobs earn between $20,000 and $75,000 a year. Many work on a freelance basis, hiring their services out to one or more clients. They may work for an hourly fee or a per-project fee and these fees may vary according to the job and the employer.

The employment outlook for writers is excellent. Although there is stiff competition for prime writing jobs, there are plenty of opportunities, particularly for those who specialize. Those who want writing careers would do well to have a specialty in addition to sharp writing skills. There will still, however, be jobs for generalists, particularly in newspaper, magazine, and book publishing. Writers who want to pursue a more creative outlet, such as novelist or poet, will encounter the same challenges as they have throughout history—stiff competition, low income, and frequent rejection. Many creative writers, however, hold other full-time writing-related jobs while they work on their more creative pursuits in their spare time.

Each article in this book discusses a particular writing occupation in detail. Many of the articles in *Careers in Focus: Writing* are similar to those in Ferguson's *Encyclopedia of Careers and Vocational Guidance,* but the articles here have been updated and revised with the latest information from the U.S. Department of Labor and other sources. The following paragraphs detail the sections and features that appear in the book.

The **Quick Facts** section provides a brief summary of the career, including recommended school subjects, personal skills, work environment, minimum educational requirements, salary ranges, certification or licensing requirements, and employment outlook. This section also provides acronyms and identification numbers for the following government classification indexes: the O*NET Dictionary of Occupational Titles (DOT), the Guide to Occupational Exploration (GOE), the National Occupational Classification (NOC) Index, and the Occupational Information Network (O*NET)-Standard Occupational Classification System (SOC) index. The DOT, GOE, and O*NET-SOC indexes have been created by the U.S. government; the NOC index is Canada's career classification system. Readers can use the identification numbers listed in the Quick Facts section to access further information about a career. Print editions of the DOT (O*NET Dictionary of Occupational Titles. Indianapolis, Ind.: JIST Works, 2004) and GOE (The Complete Guide for Occupational Exploration. Indianapolis, Ind.: JIST Works, 1993) are available at libraries. Electronic versions of the NOC (http://www23.hrdc-drhc.gc.ca) and O*NET-SOC (http://online.onetcenter.org) are available on the Internet. When no DOT, GOE, NOC, or O*NET-SOC numbers are present, this means that the U.S. Department of Labor or Human Resources Development Canada have not created a numerical designation for this career. In this instance, you will see the acronym "N/A," or not available.

The **Overview** section is a brief introductory description of the duties and responsibilities of someone in the career. Oftentimes, a career may have a variety of job titles. When this is the case, alternative career titles are presented in this section.

The **History** section describes the history of the particular job as it relates to the overall development of its industry or field.

The **Job** describes the primary and secondary duties of the job.

Requirements discusses high school and postsecondary education and training requirements, any certification or licensing necessary, and any other personal requirements for success in the job.

Exploring offers suggestions on how to gain some experience in or knowledge of the particular job before making a firm educational and financial commitment. The focus is on what can be done while still in high school (or in the early years of college) to gain a better understanding of the job.

The **Employers** section gives an overview of typical places of employment for the job.

Starting Out discusses the best ways to land that first job, be it through the college placement office, newspaper ads, or personal contact.

The **Advancement** section describes what kind of career path to expect from the job and how to get there.

Earnings lists salary ranges and describes the typical fringe benefits.

The **Work Environment** section describes the typical surroundings and conditions of employment—whether indoors or outdoors, noisy or quiet, social or independent, and so on. Also discussed are typical hours worked, any seasonal fluctuations, and the stresses and strains of the job.

The **Outlook** section summarizes the job in terms of the general economy and industry projections. For the most part, Outlook information is obtained from the Bureau of Labor Statistics and is supplemented by information taken from professional associations. Job growth terms follow those used in the *Occupational Outlook Handbook*. Growth described as "much faster than the average" means an increase of 36 percent or more. Growth described as "faster than the average" means an increase of 21 to 35 percent. Growth described as "about as fast as the average" means an increase of 10 to 20 percent. Growth described as "little change or more slowly than the average" means an increase of 0 to 9 percent. "Decline" means a decrease of 1 percent or more.

Each article ends with **For More Information**, which lists organizations that can provide career information on training, education, internships, scholarships, and job placement.

Advertising Workers

OVERVIEW

Advertising is defined as mass communication paid for by an advertiser to persuade a particular segment of the public to adopt ideas or take actions of benefit to the advertiser. *Advertising workers* perform the various creative and business activities needed to take an advertisement from the research stage, to creative concept, through production, and finally to its intended audience. There are approximately 47,000 advertising and public relations businesses in the United States, employing about 425,000 workers in 2004. The Department of Labor estimates that about 4 out of 10 of those workers write copy or are involved creatively in advertising development and production. There are 154,000 advertising sales agents, 142,000 copywriters, and 64,000 advertising and promotions managers employed in the United States.

HISTORY

Advertising has been around as long as people have been exchanging goods and services. While a number of innovations spurred the development of advertising, it wasn't until the invention of the printing press in the 15th century that merchants began posting handbills in order to advertise their goods and services. By the 19th century, newspapers became an important means of advertising, followed by magazines in the late 1800s.

One of the problems confronting merchants in the early days of advertising was where to place their ads to generate the most business. In response, a number of people emerged who specialized in

Advertising workers review the final proofs of a new print ad.
(*Corbis*)

the area of advertising, accepting ads and posting them conspicu-
ously. These agents were the first advertising workers. As competition among merchants increased, many of these agents offered to
compose ads, as well as post them, for their clients.

Today, with intense competition among both new and existing businesses, advertising has become a necessity in the marketing of goods and services alike. At the same time, the advertising worker's job has grown more demanding and complex than ever. With a wide variety of media from which advertisers can choose—including newspapers, magazines, billboards, radio, television, film and video, the World Wide Web, and a variety of other new technologies—today's advertising worker must not only develop and create ads and campaigns but keep abreast of current and developing buying and technology trends as well.

THE JOB

Approximately seven out of every 10 advertising organizations in the United States are full-service operations, offering their clients a broad range of services, including copywriting, graphics and other art-related work, production, media placement, and tracking and follow-up. These advertising agencies may have hundreds of people working in a dozen different departments, while smaller companies often employ just a handful of employees. Most agencies, however, have at least five departments: contact, research, media, creative, and production.

Contact department personnel are responsible for attracting new customers and maintaining relationships with existing ones. Heading the contact department, *advertising agency managers* are concerned with the overall activities of the company. They formulate plans to generate business, by either soliciting new accounts or getting additional business from established clients. In addition, they meet with department heads to coordinate their operations and to create policies and procedures.

Advertising account executives are the contact department employees responsible for maintaining good relations between their clients and the agency. Acting as liaisons, they represent the agency to its clients and must therefore be able to communicate clearly and effectively. After examining the advertising objectives of their clients, account executives develop campaigns or strategies and then work with others from the various agency departments to target specific audiences, create advertising communications, and execute the campaigns. Presenting concepts, as well as the ad campaign at various stages of completion, to clients for their feedback and approval, account executives must have some knowledge of overall marketing strategies and be able to sell ideas.

Working with account executives, employees in the research department gather, analyze, and interpret the information needed to make a client's advertising campaign successful. By determining who the potential buyers of a product or service will be, *research workers* predict which theme will have the most impact, what kind of packaging and price will have the most appeal, and which media will be the most effective.

Guided by a *research director*, research workers conduct local, regional, and national surveys in order to examine consumer preferences and then determine potential sales for the targeted product or service based on those preferences. Researchers also gather information about competitors' products, prices, sales, and advertising methods. To learn what the buying public prefers in a client's product over a competitor's, research workers often distribute samples and then ask the users of these samples for their opinions of the product. This information can then be used as testimonials about the product or as a means of identifying the most persuasive selling message in an ad.

Although research workers often recommend which media to use for an advertising campaign, *media planners* are the specialists who determine which print or broadcast media will be the most effective. Ultimately, they are responsible for choosing the combination of media that will reach the greatest number of potential buyers for the least amount of money, based on their clients' advertising strategies. Accordingly, planners must be familiar with the markets that each medium reaches, as well as the advantages and disadvantages of advertising in each.

Media buyers, often referred to as *space buyers* (for newspapers and magazines), or *time buyers* (for radio and television), do the actual purchasing of space and time according to a general plan formulated by the *media director*. In addition to ensuring that ads appear when and where they should, buyers negotiate costs for ad placement and maintain contact and extensive correspondence with clients and media representatives alike.

While the contact, research, and media departments handle the business side of a client's advertising campaign, the creative staff takes care of the artistic aspects. *Creative directors* oversee the activities of artists and writers and work with clients and account executives to determine the best advertising approaches, gain approval on concepts, and establish budgets and schedules.

Copywriters take the ideas submitted by creative directors and account executives and write descriptive text in the form of headlines, jingles, slogans, and other copy designed to attract the attention of potential buyers. In addition to being able to express themselves clearly and persuasively, copywriters must know what motivates people to buy. They must also be able to describe a product's features in a captivating and appealing way and be familiar with various advertising media. In large agencies, copywriters may be supervised by a *copy chief*.

Copywriters work closely with *art directors* to make sure that text and artwork create a unified, eye-catching arrangement. Planning the visual presentation of the client's message, from concept formulation to final artwork, the art director plays an important role in every stage of the creation of an advertising campaign. Art directors who work on filmed commercials and videos combine film techniques, music, and sound, as well as actors or animation, to communicate an advertiser's message. In publishing, art directors work with graphic designers, photographers, copywriters, and editors to develop brochures, catalogs, direct mail, and other printed pieces, all according to the advertising strategy.

Art directors must have a basic knowledge of graphics and design, computer software, printing, photography, and filmmaking. With the help of graphic artists, they decide where to place text and images, choose typefaces, and create storyboard ads and videos. Several layouts are usually submitted to the client, who chooses one or asks for revisions until a layout or conceptualization sketch meets with final approval. The art director then selects an illustrator, graphic artist, photographer, or TV or video producer, and the project moves on to the production department of the agency.

Production departments in large ad agencies may be divided into print production and broadcast production divisions, each with its own managers and staff. *Production managers* and their assistants convert and reproduce written copy and artwork into printed, filmed, or tape-recorded form so that they can be presented to the public. Production employees work closely with imaging, printing, engraving, and other art reproduction firms and must be familiar with various printing processes, papers, inks, typography, still and motion picture photography, digital imaging, and other processes and materials.

In addition to the principal employees in the five major departments, advertising organizations work with a variety of staff or freelance employees who have specialized knowledge, education, and skill, including photographers, photoengravers, typographers, printers, telemarketers, product and package designers, and producers of display materials. Finally, rounding out most advertising establishments are various support employees, such as production coordinators, video editors, word processors, statisticians, accountants, administrators, secretaries, and clerks.

The work of advertising employees is fast-paced, dynamic, and ever changing, depending on each client's strategies and budgets and the creative ideas generated by agency workers. In addition to innovative techniques, methods, media, and materials used by agency workers, new and emerging technologies are impacting the work of everyone in the advertising arena, from marketing executives to graphic designers. The Internet is undoubtedly the most revolutionary medium to hit the advertising scene. Through this worldwide, computer-based network, researchers are able to precisely target markets and clearly identify consumer needs. In addition, the Internet's Web pages provide media specialists with a powerful vehicle for advertising their clients' products and services. New technology has also been playing an important role in the

Technology for Advertising

Considering a career in advertising? Becoming familiar with the appropriate software can give you an edge in the job market. Though the programs themselves can be rather expensive to buy on your own, you can gain experience using them through college courses and adult-education programs.

- Adobe Photoshop: Ever wonder how so much of the eye-catching "trick photography" in today's ads is done? The answer is more than likely Adobe Photoshop, the industry-standard photo-manipulation program. Using it, you can do everything from swapping one model's head to another's body to removing stray hairs from the pictures. More than just changing photos, though, Photoshop can also subtly change lighting, add shadows, brighten color, and quickly and easily do everything that you once needed a sophisticated darkroom to accomplish. Finally, Photoshop allows you to save pictures in formats that can be used on the World Wide Web or by other design programs.

- Adobe Illustrator: Another program from Adobe, Illustrator, allows designers to create logos, make background designs, and turn text into art. Illustrator files can easily be exported and used in other programs. Because of its versatility, Illustrator is an important design tool. However, to be most effective, it requires a great deal of expertise.

- QuarkXPress: A design and layout program, Quark is used to create everything from books and magazines to single-page ads. Text and pictures can be added and swapped around, so that the ad can be designed for the maximum possible impact. Finally, Quark allows work to be exported in formats that can easily be read and set into print. Another popular design and layout program is Adobe InDesign.

creative area. Most art directors, for example, use a variety of computer software programs, and many create and oversee Web sites for their clients. Other interactive materials and vehicles, such as CD catalogs, touch screens, multidimensional visuals, and voice-mail shopping, are changing the way today's advertising workers are doing their jobs.

REQUIREMENTS

High School

You can prepare for a career as an advertising worker by taking a variety of courses at the high school level. General liberal arts courses, such as English, journalism, communications, economics, psychology, speech, business, social science, and mathematics are important for aspiring advertising employees. In addition, those interested in the creative side of the field should take such classes as art, drawing, graphic design, illustration, and art history. Finally, since computers play a vital role in the advertising field, you should become familiar with word processing and layout programs, as well as the World Wide Web.

Postsecondary Training

The American Association of Advertising Agencies notes that most agencies employing entry-level personnel prefer college graduates. Copywriters are best prepared with a college degree in English, journalism, or communications; research workers need college training in statistics, market research, and social studies; and most account executives have business or related degrees. Media positions increasingly require a college degree in communications or a technology-related area. Media directors and research directors with a master's degree have a distinct advantage over those with only an undergraduate degree. Some research department heads even have doctorates.

While the requirements from agency to agency may vary somewhat, graduates of liberal arts colleges or those with majors in fields such as communications, journalism, business administration, or marketing research are preferred. Good language skills, as well as a broad liberal arts background, are necessary for advertising workers. College students interested in the field should therefore take such courses as English, writing, art, philosophy, foreign languages, social studies, sociology, psychology, economics, mathematics, statistics, advertising, and marketing. Some 900 degree-granting institutions throughout the United States offer specialized majors in advertising as part of their curriculum.

Other Requirements

In addition to the variety of educational and work experiences neces-sary for those aspiring to advertising careers, many personal char-acteristics are also important. Although you will perform many tasks of your job independently as an advertising worker, you will also interact with others as part of a team. In addition to working with other staff members, you may be responsible for initiating and maintaining client contact. You must therefore be able to get along well with people and communicate clearly.

Advertising is not a job that involves routine, and you must be able to meet and adjust to the challenges presented by each new client and product or service. The ability to think clearly and logi-cally is important, because commonsense approaches rather than gimmicks persuade people that something is worth buying. You must also be creative, flexible, and imaginative in order to anticipate consumer demand and trends, to develop effective concepts, and to sell the ideas, products, and services of your clients.

Finally, with technology evolving at breakneck speed, it's vital that you keep pace with technological advances and trends. In addition to being able to work with the most current software and hardware, you should be familiar with the Web, as well as with other technol-ogy that is impacting—and will continue to impact—the industry.

EXPLORING

If you aspire to a career in the advertising industry, you can gain valuable insight by taking writing and art courses offered either in school or by private organizations. In addition to the theoretical ideas and techniques that such classes provide, you can actually apply what you learn by working full or part time at local depart-ment stores or newspaper offices. Some advertising agencies or research firms also employ students to interview people or to con-duct other market research. Work as an agency clerk or messenger may also be available. Participating in internships at an advertising or marketing organization is yet another way to explore the field, as well as to determine your aptitude for advertising work. You may find it helpful to read publications dedicated to this industry, such as *Advertising Age* (http://www.adage.com).

EMPLOYERS

Most advertising workers are employed by advertising agencies that plan and prepare advertising material for their clients on a commis-sion or service fee basis. However, some large companies and nearly all department stores prefer to handle their own advertising. Advertising workers in such organizations prepare advertising materials for in-house clients, such as the marketing or catalog department. They also may be involved in the planning, preparation, and production of special promotional materials, such as sales brochures, articles describing the activities of the organization, or Web sites. Some advertising workers are employed by owners of various media, including newspapers, magazines, radio and television networks, and outdoor advertising. Workers employed in these media are mainly sales representatives who sell advertising space or broadcast time to advertising agencies or companies that maintain their own advertising departments.

In addition to agencies, large companies, and department stores, advertising services and supply houses employ such advertising specialists as photographers, photoengravers, typographers, printers, product and package designers, display producers, and others who assist in the production of various advertising materials.

According to the American Association of Advertising Agencies, there are more than 13,000 advertising agencies in the United States. Most of the large firms are located in Chicago, Los Angeles, and New York. Employment opportunities are also available, however, at a variety of "small shops," four out of five of which employ fewer than 10 workers each. In addition, a growing number of self-employment and home-based business opportunities are resulting in a variety of industry jobs located in outlying areas rather than in big cities.

STARTING OUT

Although competition for advertising jobs is fierce and getting your foot in the door can be difficult, there are a variety of ways to launch a career in the field. Some large advertising agencies recruit college graduates and place them in training programs designed to acquaint beginners with all aspects of advertising work, but these opportunities are limited and highly competitive.

Instead, many graduates simply send resumes to businesses that employ entry-level advertising workers. Newspapers, radio and television stations, printers, photographers, and advertising agencies are but a few of the businesses that will hire beginners.

Those who have had work experience in sales positions often enter the advertising field as account executives. High school graduates and other people without experience who want to work in advertising, however, may find it necessary to begin as clerks or assistants to research and production staff members or to copywriters.

ADVANCEMENT

The career path in an advertising agency generally leads from trainee to skilled worker to division head and then to department head. It may also take employees from department to department, allowing them to gain more responsibility with each move. Opportunities abound for those with talent, leadership capability, and ambition.

Management positions require experience in all aspects of advertising, including agency work, communication with advertisers, and knowledge of various advertising media. Copywriters, account executives, and other advertising agency workers who demonstrate outstanding ability to deal with clients and supervise coworkers usually have a good chance of advancing to management positions. Other workers, however, prefer to acquire specialized skills. For them, advancement may mean more responsibility, the opportunity to perform more specialized tasks, and increased pay.

Advertising workers at various department stores, mail order houses, and other large firms that have their own advertising departments can also earn promotions. Advancement in any phase of advertising work is usually dependent on the employee's experience, training, and demonstrated skills.

Some qualified copywriters, artists, and account executives establish their own agencies or become marketing consultants. For these entrepreneurs, advancement may take the form of an increasing number of accounts and/or more prestigious clients.

EARNINGS

Salaries of advertising workers vary depending on the type of work, the size of the agency, its geographic location, the kind of accounts handled, and the agency's gross earnings. Salaries are also determined by a worker's education, aptitude, and experience. The wide range of jobs in advertising makes it difficult to estimate average salaries for all positions.

According to a survey by the National Association of Colleges and Employers, marketing majors entering the job market in 2005 had average starting salaries of $33,873, while advertising majors averaged $31,340.

According to a 2002 salary survey by Advertising Age, creative directors at mid-sized advertising agencies (grossing $7.6 to $15 million) earned an average of $124,000 annually. Copywriters at these agencies earned $54,000, account executives earned $47,000, and media directors made $82,000 per year. Chief Exeuctive Officers at large agencies made more than $270,000 annually, while CEOs at smaller agencies reported yearly earnings of $123,000.

The U.S. Department of Labor reports that the median annual earnings for advertising and promotions managers in 2005 were $68,860. For marketing managers the median was $92,680, sales managers earned $92,680, and public relations managers made $76,450 per year. Copywriters earned a median salary of $45,460. The lowest-paid 10 percent of advertising and promotions managers made less than $34,310, while the highest-paid marketing and sales managers earned more than $101,250.

In advertising agencies, an executive vice president can earn from $113,000 to $500,000 a year or more. Account executives earned a median of $57,188, while senior account executives earned a median of $73,329. In the research and media departments, media directors earn a median of $102,455, and media planners and buyers between $40,000 and $45,000 per year. In the creative department, art directors earn a median of $60,000 or more annually. Salaries for relatively glamorous jobs at agencies can be low, due to high competition. In advertising departments at other businesses and industries, individual earnings vary widely. Salaries of advertising workers are generally higher, however, at consumer product firms than at industrial product organizations because of the competition among consumer product producers. The majority of companies offer insurance benefits, a retirement plan, and other incentives and bonuses.

WORK ENVIRONMENT

Conditions at most agencies are similar to those found in other offices throughout the country, except that employees must frequently work under great pressure to meet deadlines. While a traditional 40-hour workweek is the norm at some companies, almost half (44 percent) of advertising, marketing, promotions, public relations, and sales managers report that they work more hours per week, including evenings and weekends. Bonuses and time off during slow periods are sometimes provided as a means of compensation for unusual workloads and hours.

Although some advertising employees, such as researchers, work independently on a great many tasks, most must function as part of a team. With frequent meetings with coworkers, clients, and media representatives alike, the work environment is usually energized, with ideas being exchanged, contracts being negotiated, and schedules being modified.

Advertising work is fast-paced and exciting. As a result, many employees often feel stressed out as they are constantly challenged to take initiative and be creative. Nevertheless, advertising workers enjoy both professional and personal satisfaction in seeing the culmination of their work communicated to sometimes millions of people.

OUTLOOK

Employment opportunities in the advertising field are expected to increase faster than the average for all industries through 2014. Demand for advertising workers will grow as a result of increased production of goods and services, both in the United States and abroad. Network and cable television, radio, newspapers, the Web, and certain other media (particularly interactive vehicles) will offer advertising workers an increasing number of employment opportunities. Some media, such as magazines, direct mail, and event marketing, are expected to provide fewer job opportunities.

Advertising agencies will enjoy faster than average employment growth, as will industries that service ad agencies and other businesses in the advertising field, such as those that offer commercial photography, imaging, art, and graphics services.

At the two extremes, enormous "mega-agencies" and small shops employing up to only 10 workers each offer employment opportunities for people with experience, talent, flexibility, and drive. In addition, self-employment and home-based businesses are on the rise. Many nonindustrial companies, such as banks, schools, and hospitals, will also be creating advertising positions.

In general, openings will become available to replace workers who change positions, retire, or leave the field for other reasons. Competition for these jobs will be keen, however, because of the large number of qualified professionals in this traditionally desirable field. Opportunities will be best for the well-qualified and well-trained applicant. Employers favor college graduates with experience, a high level of creativity, and strong communications skills. People who are not well-qualified or prepared for agency work will find the advertising field increasingly difficult to enter. The same is also true for those who seek work in companies that service ad agencies.

FOR MORE INFORMATION

For information on student chapters, scholarships, and internships, contact

American Advertising Federation
1101 Vermont Avenue, NW, Suite 500
Washington, DC 20005-6306
Tel: 202-898-0089
Email: aaf@aaf.org
http://www.aaf.org

For industry information, contact
American Association of Advertising Agencies
405 Lexington Avenue, 18th Floor
New York, NY 10174-1801
Tel: 212-682-2500
http://www.aaaa.org

For career and salary information, contact
American Marketing Association
311 South Wacker Drive, Suite 5800
Chicago, IL 60606-6629
Tel: 800-262-1150
http://www.marketingpower.com

The Art Directors Club is an international, nonprofit organization for creatives in advertising, graphic design, interactive media, broadcast design, typography, packaging, environmental design, photography, illustration, and related disciplines.
Art Directors Club
106 West 29th Street
New York, NY 10001-5301
Tel: 212-643-1440
Email: info@adcny.org
http://www.adcglobal.org

For information on student membership and careers, contact
Direct Marketing Educational Foundation
1120 Avenue of the Americas
New York, NY 10036-6700
Tel: 212-768-7277
http://www.the-dma.org

The Graphic Artists Guild promotes and protects the economic interests of the artist/designer and is committed to improving conditions for all creators of graphic art and raising standards for the entire industry.
Graphic Artists Guild
32 Broadway, Suite 1114
New York, NY 10004-1612
Tel: 212-791-3400
http://www.gag.org

Columnists

QUICK FACTS

School Subjects
Computer science
English
Journalism

Personal Skills
Communication/ideas
Helping/teaching

Work Environment
Indoors and outdoors
Primarily multiple locations

Minimum Education Level
Bachelor's degree

Salary Range
$18,300 to $32,270 to
$71,220+

Certification or Licensing
None available

Outlook
More slowly than the average

DOT
131

GOE
01.03.01

NOC
5123

O*NET-SOC
27-3022.00

OVERVIEW

Columnists write opinion pieces for publication in newspapers or magazines. Some columnists work for syndicates, which are organizations that sell articles to many media at once.

Columnists can be generalists who write about whatever strikes them on any topic. Most columnists, however, focus on a specialty, such as government, politics, local issues, health, humor, sports, gossip, or other themes.

Most newspapers employ local columnists or run columns from syndicates. Some syndicated columnists work out of their homes or private offices.

HISTORY

Because the earliest American newspapers were political vehicles, much of their news stories brimmed with commentary and opinion. This practice continued up until the Civil War. Horace Greeley, a popular editor who had regularly espoused partisanship in his *New York Tribune*, was the first to give editorial opinion its own page separate from the news.

As newspapers grew into instruments of mass communication, their editors sought balance and fairness on the editorial pages and began publishing a number of columns with varying viewpoints.

Famous Washington, D.C.-based columnist Jack Anderson was known for bringing an investigative slant to the editorial page. Art Buchwald and Molly Ivins became well known for their satirical look at government and politicians.

The growth of news and commentary on the Internet has only added to the power of columnists.

THE JOB

Columnists often take news stories and enhance the facts with personal opinions and panache. Columnists may also write from their personal experiences. Either way, a column usually has a punchy start, a pithy middle, and a strong, sometimes poignant, ending.

Columnists are responsible for writing columns on a regular basis on accord with a schedule, depending on the frequency of publication. They may write a column daily, weekly, quarterly, or monthly. Like other journalists, they face pressure to meet deadlines.

Most columnists are free to select their own story ideas. The need to constantly come up with new and interesting ideas may be one of the hardest parts of the job, but also one of the most rewarding. Columnists search through newspapers, magazines, and the Internet, watch television, and listen to the radio. The various types of media suggest ideas and keep the writer aware of current events and social issues.

Next, they do research, delving into a topic much like an investigative reporter would, so that they can back up their arguments with facts.

Finally, they write, usually on a computer. After a column is written, at least one editor goes over it to check for clarity and to correct mistakes. Then the cycle begins again. Often a columnist will write a few relatively timeless pieces to keep for use as backups in a pinch, in case a new idea can't be found or falls through.

Most columnists work in newsrooms or magazine offices, although some, especially those who are syndicated but not affiliated with a particular newspaper, work out of their homes or private offices. Many well-known syndicated columnists work out of Washington, D.C.

Newspapers often run small pictures of columnists, called head shots, next to their columns. This, and a consistent placement of a column in a particular spot in the paper, usually gives a columnist greater recognition than a reporter or editor.

REQUIREMENTS

High School

You'll need a broad-based education to do this job well, so take a college prep curriculum in high school. Concentrate on English and journalism classes that will help you develop research and writing skills. Keep your computer skills up to date with computer science courses. History, psychology, science, and math should round out your education. Are you interested in a particular topic, such as sports, politics, or developments in medicine? Then take classes that will help you develop your knowledge in that area. In the future, you'll be able to draw on this knowledge when you write your column.

Postsecondary Training

As is the case for other journalists, at least a bachelor's degree in journalism is usually required, although some journalists graduate with degrees in political science or English. Experience may be gained by writing for the college or university newspaper and through a summer internship at a newspaper or other publication. It also may be helpful to submit freelance opinion columns to local or national publications. The more published articles, called *clips*, you can show to prospective employers, the better.

Other Requirements

Being a columnist requires similar characteristics to those required for being a reporter: curiosity, a genuine interest in people, the ability to write clearly and succinctly, and the strength to thrive under deadline pressure. But as a columnist, you will also require a certain wit and wisdom, the compunction to express strong opinions, and the ability to take apart an issue and debate it.

EXPLORING

A good way to explore this career is to work for your school newspaper and perhaps write your own column. Participation in debate clubs

What Is a Blog?

A "blog"—short for "Web log"—is a sort of journal put up for public viewing on the World Wide Web. The first blogs, arguably, were the "plan files" attached to old text-based Internet accounts. Users frequently kept personal information, from their hobbies to their evening's plans, in these files. With the growth of the World Wide Web, many people took the opportunity to put their thoughts on the Web. Improved technology has made it increasingly easy to create and update a Web site. Most people use their blogs to share their day-to-day personal experiences with friends, family, and anyone who happens by. However, some amateur and professional journalists have used the power of blogging to self-publish their own newspaper columns. Not only has blogging become an indicator of popular opinion that mainstream journalists, editors, and politicians have been forced to pay attention to, but with many sensitively-placed people anonymously keeping their own publicly accessible online diaries, blogs have become an important source of "hard" news, as well.

will help you form opinions and express them clearly. Read your city's newspaper regularly, and take a look at national papers as well as magazines. Which columnists, on the local and national level, interest you? Why do you feel their columns are well done? Try to incorporate good qualities you observe into your own writing. Contact your local newspaper and ask for a tour of the facilities. This will give you a sense of what the office atmosphere is like and what technologies are used there. Ask to speak with one of the paper's regular columnists about his or her job. He or she may be able to provide you with valuable insights. Visit the Dow Jones Newspaper Fund Web site (http://djnewspaperfund.dowjones.com/fund) for information on careers, summer programs, internships, and more. Try getting a part-time or summer job at the newspaper, even if it's just answering phones and doing data entry. In this way you'll be able to test out how well you like working in such an atmosphere.

EMPLOYERS

Newspapers of all kinds run columns, as do certain magazines and even public radio stations, where a tape is played over the airways of the author reading the column. Some columnists are self-employed, preferring to market their work to syndicates instead of working for a single newspaper or magazine.

STARTING OUT

Most columnists start out as reporters. Experienced reporters are the ones most likely to become columnists. Occasionally, however, a relatively new reporter may suggest a weekly column if the beat being covered warrants it, for example, politics.

Another route is to start out by freelancing, sending columns out to a multitude of newspapers and magazines in the hopes that someone will pick them up. Also, columns can be marketed to syndicates. A list of these, and magazines that may also be interested in columns, is provided in the Writer's Market (http://www.writersmarket.com).

A third possibility, one opened up by the Internet, is simply beginning your own site or blog and using it to attract attention and thus jumpstart your career. Many columnists who are well known, such as Matt Drudge (http://www.drudgereport.com) and "Wonkette" (http://www.wonkette.com), started by beginning their own Web columns. If you get scoops, run interesting content, and people like what you have to say, you may find yourself with more readers than you can handle.

ADVANCEMENT

Newspaper columnists can advance in national exposure by having their work syndicated. They also may try to get a collection of their columns published in book form. Moving from a small newspaper or magazine to a large national publication is another way to advance.

Columnists also may choose to work in other editorial positions, such as editor, editorial writer or page editor, or foreign correspondent.

EARNINGS

Like reporters' salaries, the incomes of columnists vary greatly according to experience, newspaper size and location, and whether the columnist is under a union contract. But generally, columnists earn higher salaries than reporters.

The U.S. Department of Labor classifies columnists with news analysts, reporters, and correspondents, and reports that the median annual income for these professionals was $32,270 in 2005. Ten percent of those in this group earned less than $18,300, and 10 percent made more than $71,220 annually. According to the Annual Survey of Journalism & Mass Communication Graduates, directed by the University of Georgia, the median salary for those who graduated in 2004 with bachelor's degrees in journalism or mass communication was $27,800. Median earnings varied somewhat by employer; for example, those working for weekly papers earned somewhat less, while those working for consumer magazines earned somewhat more. Although these salary figures are for all journalists (not just columnists), they provide a general range for those working in this field. However, popular columnists at large papers earn considerably higher salaries.

Freelancers may get paid by the column. Syndicates pay columnists 40 percent to 60 percent of the sales income generated by their columns or a flat fee if only one column is being sold.

Freelancers must provide their own benefits. Columnists working on staff at newspapers and magazines receive typical benefits such as health insurance, paid vacation days, sick days, and retirement plans.

WORK ENVIRONMENT

Columnists work mostly indoors in newspaper or magazine offices, although they may occasionally conduct interviews or do research on location out of the office. Some columnists may work as much as 48 to 52 hours a week. Some columnists do the majority of their writing at home or in a private office, and come to the newsroom primarily for meetings and to have their work approved or changed by editors. The atmosphere in a newsroom is generally fast paced and loud, so columnists must be able to concentrate and meet deadlines in this type of environment.

OUTLOOK

The U.S. Department of Labor predicts that employment for news analysts, reporters, and correspondents (including columnists) will grow more slowly than the average for all occupations through 2014. Growth will be hindered by such factors as mergers and closures of newspapers, decreasing circulation, and lower profits from advertising revenue. Online publications may be a source for new jobs. Competition for newspaper and magazine positions is very competitive, and competition for the position of columnist is even stiffer because these are prestigious jobs that are limited in number. Smaller daily and weekly newspapers may be easier places to find employment than major metropolitan newspapers, and movement up the ladder to columnist will also likely be quicker. Pay, however, is less than at bigger papers. Journalism and mass communication graduates will have the best opportunities, and writers will be needed to replace those who leave the field for other work or retire.

FOR MORE INFORMATION

For a list of accredited programs in journalism and mass communications, visit the ACEJMC Web site:
Accrediting Council on Education in Journalism and Mass
   Communications (ACEJMC)
University of Kansas School of Journalism and Mass
   Communications
Stauffer-Flint Hall, 1435 Jayhawk Boulevard
Lawrence, KS 66045-7575
Tel: 785-864-3973
http://www2.ku.edu/~acejmc/student/student.shtml

For information on careers in newspaper reporting, education, and financial aid opportunities, contact
American Society of Journalists and Authors
1501 Broadway, Suite 302
New York, NY 10036-5505

Tel: 212-997-0947
http://www.asja.org

This association provides general educational information on all areas of journalism, including newspapers, magazines, television, and radio.
Association for Education in Journalism and Mass Communication
234 Outlet Pointe Boulevard
Columbia, SC 29210-5667
Tel: 803-798-0271
http://www.aejmc.org

For information on jobs, scholarships, internships, college programs, and other resources, contact
National Association of Broadcasters
1771 N Street, NW
Washington, DC 20036-2800
Tel: 202-429-5300
Email: nab@nab.org
http://www.nab.org

The SPJ has student chapters all over the United States and offers information on scholarships and internships.
Society of Professional Journalists (SPJ)
3909 North Meridian Street
Indianapolis, IN 46208-4011
Tel: 317-927-8000
http://www.spj.org

Visit the following Web site for comprehensive information on journalism careers, summer programs, and college journalism programs.
High School Journalism
http://www.highschooljournalism.org

Comic Book Writers

OVERVIEW

Comic book writers create and develop characters, stories, and plots for comic books. Comic book writers may have an idea for an entirely new comic book, or they may think of stories and plots for an existing comic book series or character.

HISTORY

The origin of comic books dates back to newspaper comic strips that first gained popularity in the United States in 1895, when Richard F. Outcault's "The Yellow Kid" appeared in the *New York World*. The huge success of this strip led to merchandise licensing, stage adaptations, and so forth, all revolving around the strip's lead character, a pushy, colorful slum youth. Because "The Yellow Kid" was so profitable, it led others to create such competing strips as "The Katzenjammer Kids," "Little Jimmy," "Barney Google," and "Toonerville Folks." These offerings appeared weekdays in newspapers around the country (usually in black-and-white artwork and often in color for the weekend entries).

Meanwhile in the early 1900s newsstands across America were filled increasingly with pulp magazines (which gained their name because they were published on low-cost, coarse pulp paper). They often featured trashy, and sometimes lurid, short fiction. Compared to more costly hardback books, pulp publications were geared to be inexpensive, quick and simple to read, and disposable. The sensational pulp stories—including such standout examples as the jungle adventures of Tarzan of the Apes and the outer space exploits of Buck Rog-

QUICK FACTS

School Subjects
Art
English
Journalism

Personal Skills
Artistic
Communication/ideas

Work Environment
Primarily indoors
Primarily one location

Minimum Education Level
High school diploma

Salary Range
$24,320 to $46,420 to $89,940+

Certification or Licensing
None available

Outlook
About as fast as the average

DOT
131

GOE
01.01.02

NOC
5121

O*NET-SOC
27-3043.00, 27-3043.02

ers— developed quite a strong public following, especially in the post-World War I period of the 1920s and early 1930s.

After pulp fiction magazines became an established reading tradition, a new twist came along in 1933. Harry Wildenberg and Max C. Gaines, who worked for the Eastern Color Printing Company, came up with the idea of a 32-page booklet that would reprint Sunday comic strips in splashy colors. (There had been some earlier efforts to reprint comic strips in black and white editions, but they lacked the new convenient format or newsstand distribution to be very successful.) When this first offering—entitled *Funnies on Parade*—was sold to Proctor & Gamble to be used as a promotional giveaway, it was an instant hit. Wildenberg and Gaines began to sell other such comic reprint collections on the nation's newsstands at a reasonable 10-cent price tag.

By 1935 Major Malcolm Wheeler-Nicholson, a one-time U.S. cavalry officer and a previous writer of pulp stories, entered the expanding field. He came up with the notion of publishing original comic strips in several panels that made up a short story-length episode. His initial publication was *New Fun Comics*, an anthology of assorted comic strip narratives featuring entries in the humor, Western, and adventure veins. In 1937 Wheeler-Nicholson formed Detective Comics Inc. (the firm that later changed its name to DC Comics) with two partners, Harry Donnerfield and Jack Liebowitz. The latter two soon bought out the financially strapped Wheeler-Nicholson and, in 1938, published a new comic book, *Action Comics #1*. This entry featured a man of steel who strode and flew about in his red-and-blue costume, helping people in distress. He was known as Superman.

The ongoing adventures of the amazing Superman proved so popular with readers that, before long, each monthly issue of *Action Comics* was selling over 1.25 million copies. (A similar triumph was enjoyed by Detective Comics' next big comic book property, Batman, another fantastic costumed avenger of wrong who boasted a sidekick, Robin. Like Superman, Batman and Robin had secret real-life identities.) These major successes induced several other businessmen to rush into the profitable field. Within a few years there were nearly 170 different comic book entries being published on a frequent basis. By now there was an established tradition that comic book artists and writers were paid a page rate (typically around $10 per page) and that ownership of the characters and stories belonged to the publishers (who made and kept all the big profits).

The creation of Superman in 1938 ushered in the Golden Age of Comic Books. This period lasted until the mid-1950s. Comic books were extremely popular during this time and many superheroes made their debut and dominated the medium. During World War II the comic book industry was booming. By 1943 more than 25 million comic books were being sold monthly. After the war, business was still thriving for the whole comic book industry. Although superhero comics were still popular, they had lost their novelty and edge through overexposure, especially from the many low-caliber rip-offs that filled the newsstand racks. Now the latest hot trends in the ever-changing comic book business were romance tales, crime dramas, Western adventures, and women's stories.

During the 1950s, the comic book trade began to realize the great changes that the end of World War II brought to the industry. With millions of servicemen returning home after the war, the U.S. government was no longer ordering and shipping tons of comic books to the armed forces abroad. Once reestablished into civilian life, the flood of ex-G.I.s no longer had the time or spare money to spend on comic books. This loss of comic book readership kept mounting as the 1940s ended.

Also by the late 1940s, commercial television was becoming increasingly popular in the United States as TV sets became more affordable. Former comic book buyers/readers suddenly became glued to the small screen, where they could watch entertainment for free. Adding to the industry's problems was the fact that there were so many established and new comic books flooding the newsstands that the average reader was becoming overwhelmed with the variety of products. Many of these books seemed (and often were) a rehash of what had been published previously in one form or another.

The comic book business also had its share of hard times with censorship. Going back to the early 1900s, civic groups were already protesting newspaper comic strips, which they claimed promoted unruly behavior on the part of the readers—especially children. The argument that comics had a negative moral impact was revived in the 1930s. Then it was argued that the comic-strip capers of "Dick Tracy" and "Terry and the Pirates" were far too racy for innocent youngsters.

Another serious threat to the comic-strip/comic book business occurred in the spring of 1940, when newspaper writer Sterling North wrote the article "A National Disgrace" in the *Chicago Daily News*. This lengthy article argued that comics were helping to ruin the morality and cultural standards of school children. It led to the formation of many parents groups around the nation who lobbied against the ill effects of comics. In reaction, a few publishers, such as *Parents Magazine*'s *True Comics* (1941), began to focus on very wholesome characters and bland story lines in their upcoming books. As World War II became a growing reality to

Americans, however, the anti-comic book campaign faded—for the time being—and things were much as before within the industry.

After World War II, censorship groups again gained strength and launched campaigns about the bad effects of most comic books on youth. In reaction to this rising tide against the comic book business, some publishers banded together to create a self-censorship organization, the Comics Magazine Association of America (CMAA). They assured the angry protest groups that their new, sanitized product was not damaging the minds and morals of America's youth. Despite the anti-censorship efforts of the industry, the attacks against comic books reached new heights. In April 1954 the U.S. Senate formed a subcommittee to examine the dangers in the contents of comic books to formative minds. The CMAA established a code to control the contents of their publications. Among the rules established was one that attempted to tone down any examples of violence. Such guidelines made it difficult for writers to present comic book characters, plot, and dialogue in the ways they had in the past.

As the CMAA's code was implemented throughout the industry, comic books became bland and limited in variation. As a result, the public was far less interested in the once exciting medium. Sales of comic books tumbled. By the late 1940s and early 1950s, superhero comics had gone out of fashion, largely replaced by comics in genres such as romance, women's stories, and Westerns.

Sales and popularity of comic books reemerged with the Silver Age of Comics in the early 1960s. There was a resurgence of superheroes and they became more human and troubled as their characters evolved. Marvel Comics was a dominating publisher. In 1961 Marvel sold 7 million copies of its books; the next year their circulation increased to 13 million. The Silver Age lasted until the early 1970s. During the 1970s the CMAA code was gradually relaxed and eventually dropped. The Silver Age was followed by The Bronze Age (early 1970s to mid-1980s) and the Modern Age (mid-1980s until present).

THE JOB

Like all those who work with the written word, comic book writers are first and foremost good communicators. Specifically, comic book writers are creative storytellers who possess both a strong command of language and a good visual sense. Although comic book writers do not have to be (and often are not) good visual artists, they must be able to weave engaging stories that can be rendered in lively artwork and told within a limited number of comic book panels. These challenges are unique to comic book writers, but it is a love of these challenges and the comic book form that attracts writers to this field.

Comic book writing, like all creative processes, starts with an idea. Writers may have an idea for an entirely new comic book, or they may think of stories and plots for an existing comic book series or character. Developing strong characters is one of the essential steps in creating a good comic book story, especially if the characters will be part of a comic book series. Before writing a specific plot, a comic book writer develops an in-depth profile and backstory for the main character. For example, one of the most popular types of comic book characters is the superhero. Among other things, the writer must decide on the hero's background, general physical appearance (both as a superhero and as an everyday citizen, if the character has such a dual nature), powers (and how they came to be), weaknesses or flaws, enemies, love interests, costume, day job, means of transport, and so forth. In addition, the writer will invent a cast of recurring minor characters, such as a wisecracking boss, nosy neighbor, or faithful sidekick. The writer must also carefully plan the setting of the comic book (urban metropolis, another planet, medieval times, and so forth). A writer's careful consideration of even the smallest details will make a comic book that much more engaging and believable for readers—even if it is primarily a fantastic tale. Working out these details will also make it easier for a writer to communicate his or her ideas to the comic book artists (called pencillers and inkers) who will actually draw the story.

After writers have developed the main character and the "world" of the comic book, they can begin to focus on stories and plots. Sometimes writers come up with these ideas through genuine inspiration, but stories for established comic book series are often the result of a brainstorming session between writers and comic book editors. (Among other things, editors come up with story ideas; evaluate ideas from freelance writers and artists; review the art and language used in comic books; and ensure continuity of character, plot, and visuals within one volume or across a comic book series.) In such a session, writers and editors come up with as many ideas as they can, no matter how outlandish some might seem. They will then go back over the list of ideas and accept, reject, and refine them until they arrive at an agreed-upon list of workable stories. They will also determine if the story will be contained in one volume or if it will be a miniseries that continues across several volumes.

A writer who is not established with a comic book publisher can also submit story ideas. He or she presents the idea in a log line, which is a one-line story summary, or in a lengthier synopsis, which is a one- or two-page summary of a story that contains the major events, some key lines of text, and brief descriptions of subplots. A synopsis is often the preferred method, as it provides more detail and makes it easier for artists to get a sense of how the action will unfold across the pages.

Space is at a premium in comics, so a writer must determine how to best convey the story, that is, how many panels will be used per page, and how many of those panels will contain text. There is no set limit to the number of panels than can appear on a page; in fact, the number of panels per page in one comic book usually varies. For example, a conversation between two people might take up 10 panels on one page, while a big action sequence might only require one or two panels. (The splash page, the first page in a comic book, is often rather elaborately drawn and thus consists of one panel.) The writer works closely with the comic book artists when making these kinds of decisions.

Comic books writers employ two main forms of writing: captions and dialogue. Captions, which usually appear as boxes in the margins of a panel, are used to convey the passage of time ("Later that day . . ."), setting ("Meanwhile, back at the lab . . ."), and mood ("In the Golden Age of Planet Xon, even the sun shone brighter."). Dialogue generally appears in bubbles or balloons near the character that is speaking. These balloons may also show a character's internal thoughts, which are usually drawn differently to distinguish them from dialogue. A writer must handle dialogue carefully, as too many balloons on one page can confuse the reader. (The accepted rule of thumb is no more than three balloons per panel.)

A writer presents his or her story to an editor or artists in one of three ways: as a storyboard, as a script, or by writing text after the art has been created. In a storyboard, the writer makes a rough layout of the text and art by drawing crude comic book panels with stick figures or basic art and the text in its proper place. This gives the artist a specific idea of how the action will unfold and how many panels the writer had in mind. When creating a comic book script, a writer also does a panel-by-panel breakdown of the story and action, but uses only words to do so. For example, a comic book script would contain pages labeled "Page 3-Panel 4" and "Page 3-Panel 5." Each page contains the clearly labeled captions, art directions, and dialogue for that panel.

In some instances the comic book artist will draw all of the artwork for the book based on the writer's original synopsis. This works especially well in comics where action and plot are emphasized over dialogue and captions. In this scenario, once the panels have been drawn, the writer will create text that corresponds to the action.

Comic book writers can be employed either as in-house staff or as freelancers. Pay varies according to experience and the position, but freelancers must provide their own office space and equipment such as computers and fax machines. Freelancers also are responsible for keeping tax records, sending out invoices, negotiating contracts, and providing their own health insurance.

REQUIREMENTS

High School

While in high school, build a broad educational foundation by taking courses in English, literature, foreign languages, history, general science, social studies, and computer science. Take art classes, as well, as these will help you understand the artistic skills and visual sense needed to create a comic book.

Postsecondary Training

Although obtaining a college degree is not required to become a comic book writer, it may give you an advantage if you apply for a writing or editorial position in the small and competitive comic book field. In addition, many comic book writers cannot make a living in comic books alone and thus hold full-time positions in other writing and non-writing fields. Having a college degree will benefit you in this respect, as well. Many comic book writers have a broad liberal arts background or majors in English, art, literature, history, philosophy, or social sciences. A number of schools offer courses in journalism, and some of them offer courses or majors in book publishing, publication management, and newspaper and magazine writing, which could be useful in preparing for work in this field

Most comic book publishers look for writers with proven writing experience. If you have served on high school or college newspapers, yearbooks, or literary magazines, or if you have worked for small community newspapers or radio stations, even in an unpaid position, you will be an attractive candidate. Many book publishers, magazines, newspapers, and radio and television stations have summer internship programs that provide valuable training in this regard. Interns do many simple tasks, such as running errands and answering phones, but some may be asked to perform research, conduct interviews, or even write some minor pieces.

Other Requirements

To be a comic book writer, you should be creative and able to express ideas clearly, have a broad general knowledge and a good sense of visual and literary storytelling, be skilled in research techniques, and be computer literate. Other assets include curiosity, persistence, initiative, resourcefulness, an accurate memory, and, of course, a good knowledge of the different styles of comic books. As with most jobs that involve publishing, the ability to concentrate, work under pressure, and meet deadlines is essential for a comic book writer.

EXPLORING

The best advice for a budding comic book writer is to become as familiar with different styles of comics and stories as possible. Read about the history of comics, observing how they and the public's tastes in them have changed over the decades. See what types of stories were quick fads and which have stood the test of time. Read and reread different styles of comics and see how the writers have developed characters, mood, setting, and continuity across issues. Attend local and national comic book conventions and talk to people working in the field. Ask how they got their start in the business and think about how you might go about getting your feet wet in this industry.

Most writers are also voracious readers. In addition to reading comic books, read novels, plays, memoirs, and biographies to learn the different ways in which writers handle character, plot, dialogue, and setting. Start to develop some of your own comic worlds, characters, and stories by fleshing out the details of each.

You can develop your sense of visual storytelling by visiting museums and seeing paintings that capture various actions, moods, and expressions. Practice storyboarding some of your own comic book ideas to gain a sense of what works in the confines of the comic book page and what does not.

Finally, you can test your interest and aptitude in the field of writing by serving as a reporter or writer on school newspapers, yearbooks, and literary magazines. Various writing courses and workshops will provide the opportunity to sharpen your writing skills.

EMPLOYERS

There are approximately 142,000 writers and authors currently employed in the United States, a small percentage of which are comic book writers. Comic book writers are employed by the two largest comic book publishers, Marvel and DC, and by smaller comic publishers, book publishers who publish graphic novels, and humor and pop culture magazines. In many instances, comic book writers make a living by working on a freelance or part-time basis for several of these types of publications.

Full-time writers also work for advertising agencies and public relations firms and work on journals and newsletters published by business and nonprofit organizations, such as professional associations, labor unions, and religious organizations. Other employers are government agencies and film production companies.

STARTING OUT

There is no one path to becoming a comic book writer, but a fair amount of experience is required to gain a high-level position in the comic book field. Some writers start out in entry-level positions at comic book publishers as assistants or interns, which are sometimes unpaid positions. An assistant may at first be asked to sit in on brainstorming sessions to get a feel for how new ideas are decided upon. He or she may gradually be given more responsibility or input on new comic book projects, which might include some writing responsibilities.

In many cases comic book writers are simply comic fans who diligently submit their proposals and synopses to established comic book publishers in the hopes of eventually getting an acceptance letter. Others pool resources with other talented friends and produce and distribute their own comic books with the hopes of eventually finding an audience. In any scenario, it is important to learn as much as possible about the workings of the comic book industry and to form a substantial portfolio of ideas and writing samples. Showing that you can tackle various comic genres (such as action, horror, comedy, drama, romance, and science fiction) will showcase for publishers your creativity and versatility as a writer.

ADVANCEMENT

Many comic book writers find their first jobs as interns or editorial or production assistants. Promotion into more responsible positions and full-scale writing responsibilities comes with diligence and experience. Freelance or self-employed writers earn advancement in the form of larger fees as they gain exposure and establish their reputations.

EARNINGS

In 2005, median annual earnings for salaried writers and authors were $46,420 a year, according to the Bureau of Labor Statistics. The lowest-paid 10 percent earned less than $24,320, while the highest-paid 10 percent earned $89,940 or more. Freelance comic book writers may earn from $5,000 to $15,000 a year. Full-time established freelance comic book writers may earn up to $75,000 a year.

WORK ENVIRONMENT

Working conditions for comic book writers range from the comforts of home to a regular office environment, depending on whether the writer works full or part time and the type of comic book publisher for which he or she works. A few of the larger comic book publishers are housed in large offices in major U.S. cities, but most are modest operations that are located in small offices and, in some cases, in private homes. Many comic book writers start their careers and build their portfolios by writing in their leisure time after work or school.

Comic book writing, like all writing, can be arduous, but most writers are seldom bored. The most difficult element is the continual pressure of deadlines. People who are the most content as writers enjoy and work well with deadline pressure.

OUTLOOK

The employment of writers is expected to increase at an average rate through 2014, according to the U.S. Department of Labor. Competition for writing jobs has been and will continue to be keen, especially in the small and highly competitive field of comic books. The comic book industry has seen many ups and downs over the past several decades, with the age and demographics of comic book readers shifting to older, more discriminating audiences. Graphic novels and comics for older audiences are gaining popularity around the world, which has opened up more vistas for comic book writers in terms of style and theme. Although finding work in the comic book industry can be challenging, doing so is rewarding on many levels for the comic book writer who displays creativity, versatility, and a true passion for the medium itself.

FOR MORE INFORMATION

For the latest news in the comic book industry and links to comics Web sites, visit the following sites:

Comic Book Industry Alliance
http://www.thecbia.com/index2.html

Comic Book Resources
http://www.comicbookresources.com

Desktop Publishing Specialists

OVERVIEW

Desktop publishing specialists prepare reports, brochures, books, cards, and other documents for printing. They create computer files of text, graphics, and page layout. They work with files others have created, or they compose original text and graphics for clients. There are approximately 34,000 desktop publishing specialists employed in the United States.

HISTORY

When Johannes Gutenberg invented movable type in the 1440s, it was a major technological advancement. Up until that point, books were produced entirely by monks, every word written by hand on vellum. Though print shops flourished all across Europe with this invention, inspiring the production of millions of books by the 1500s, there was little major change in the technology of printing until the 1800s. By then, cylinder presses were churning out thousands of sheets per hour, and the Linotype machine allowed for easier, more efficient plate-making. Offset lithography (a method of applying ink from a treated surface onto paper) followed and gained popularity after World War II. Phototypesetting was later developed, involving creating film images of text and pictures to be printed. At the end of the 20th century, computers caused another revolution in the industry. Laser printers now allow for low-cost, high-quality printing, and desktop publishing software is credited with spurring sales and use of personal home computers.

Eric Eldred of Eldritch Press uses a flatbed scanner to scan old books into digital files. After scanning the books are made available to readers who visit the company's Web site. *(Christopher Fitzgerald/The Image Works)*

THE JOB

If you have ever used a computer to design and print a page in your high school paper or yearbook, then you've had some experience in desktop publishing. Not so many years ago, the prepress process (the steps to prepare a document for the printing press) involved metal casts, molten lead, light tables, knives, wax, paste, and a number of different professionals from artists to typesetters. With computer technology, these jobs are becoming more consolidated.

Desktop publishing specialists have artistic talents, proofreading skills, sales and marketing abilities, and a great deal of computer knowledge. They work on computers converting and preparing files for printing presses and other media, such as the Internet and CD-ROM. Much of desktop publishing is called prepress, when specialists typeset, or arrange and transform, text and graphics. They use the latest in design software; programs such as PhotoShop, Illustrator, InDesign, PageMaker (all from software designer Adobe), and QuarkXpress, are the most popular. Some desktop publishing specialists also use CAD (computer-aided design) technology, allowing them to create images and effects with a digitizing pen.

Once they have created a file to be printed, desktop publishing specialists either submit it to a commercial printer or print the pieces themselves. Whereas traditional typesetting costs over $20 per page, desktop printing can cost less than a penny a page. Individuals hire the services of desktop publishing specialists for creating and printing invitations, advertising and fundraising brochures, newsletters, flyers, and business cards. Commercial printing involves catalogs, brochures, and reports, while business printing encompasses products used by businesses, such as sales receipts and forms.

Typesetting and page layout work entails selecting font types and sizes, arranging column widths, checking for proper spacing between letters, words, and columns, placing graphics and pictures, and more. Desktop publishing specialists choose from the hundreds of typefaces available, taking the purpose and tone of the text into consideration when selecting from fonts with round shapes or long shapes, thick strokes or thin, serifs or sans serifs. Editing is also an important duty of a desktop publishing specialist. Articles must be updated, or in some cases rewritten, before they are arranged on a page. As more people use their own desktop publishing programs to create print-ready files, desktop publishing specialists will have to be even more skillful at designing original work and promoting their professional expertise to remain competitive.

Darryl Gabriel and his wife Maree own a desktop publishing service in Australia. The Internet has allowed them to publicize the business globally. They currently serve customers in their local area and across Australia, and are hoping to expand more into international Internet marketing. The Gabriels use a computer ("But one is not enough," Darryl says), a laser printer, and a scanner to create business cards, pamphlets, labels, books, and personalized greeting cards. Though they must maintain computer skills, they also have a practical understanding of the equipment. "We keep our prices down by being able to re-ink our cartridges," Darryl says. "This takes a little getting used to at first, but once you get a knack for it, it becomes easier."

Desktop publishing specialists deal with technical issues, such as resolution problems, colors that need to be corrected, and software difficulties. A client may come in with a hand-drawn sketch, a printout of a design, or a file on a diskette, and he or she may want the piece ready to be posted on the Internet or to be published in a high-quality brochure, newspaper, or magazine. Each format presents different issues, and desktop publishing specialists must be familiar with the processes and solutions for each. They may also provide services such as color scanning, laminating, image manipulation, and poster production.

Customer relations are as important as technical skills. Darryl Gabriel encourages desktop publishing specialists to learn how to use equipment and software to their fullest potential. He also advises them to know their customers. "Try and be as helpful as possible to your customers," he says, "so you can provide them with products that they are happy with and that are going to benefit their businesses." He says it is also very important to follow up, calling customers to make sure they are pleased with the work. "If you're able to relate to what the customers want, and if you encourage them to be involved in the initial design process, then they'll be confident they're going to get quality products."

REQUIREMENTS

High School

Classes that will help you develop desktop publishing skills include computer classes and design and art classes. Computer classes should include both hardware and software, since understanding how computers function will help you with troubleshooting and knowing the capabilities and limits of a computer. Through photography classes you can learn about composition, color, and design elements. Typing, drafting, and print shop classes, if available, will also provide you with the opportunity to gain some indispensable skills. Working on the school newspaper or yearbook will train you on desktop publishing skills as well, including page layout, typesetting, composition, and working under a deadline.

Postsecondary Training

Although a college degree is not a prerequisite, many desktop publishing specialists have at least a bachelor's degree. Areas of study range anywhere from English to graphic design. Some two-year colleges and technical institutes offer programs in desktop publishing or related fields. A growing number of schools offer programs in technical and visual communications, which may include classes in desktop publishing, layout and design, and computer graphics. Four-year colleges also offer courses in technical communications and graphic design. You can enroll in classes related to desktop publishing through extended education programs offered through universities and colleges. These classes, often taught by professionals in the industry, cover basic desktop publishing techniques and advanced lessons on Adobe Photoshop, InDesign, or QuarkXPress.

Certification or Licensing

Certification is not mandatory; currently there is only one certification program offered in desktop publishing. The Association of Graphic Communications has an electronic publishing certificate designed to set industry standards and measure the competency levels of desktop publishing specialists. The examination is divided into a written portion and a hands-on portion. During the practical exam, candidates receive files on a disk and must manipulate images and text, make color corrections, and perform whatever tasks are necessary to create the final product. Applicants are expected to be knowledgeable in print production, color separation, typography and font management, computer hardware and software, image manipulation, page layout, scanning and color correcting, prepress and pre-flighting, and output device capabilities.

Other Requirements

Desktop publishing specialists are detail-oriented, possess problem-solving skills, and have a sense of design and artistic skills. "People tell me I have a flair for graphic design and mixing the right color with the right graphics," Darryl Gabriel says.

A good eye and patience are critical, as well as endurance to see projects through to the finish. You should have an aptitude for computers, the ability to type quickly and accurately, and a natural curiosity. In addition, a calm temperament comes in handy when working under pressure and constant deadlines. You should be flexible and be able to handle more than one project at a time.

EXPLORING

Experimenting with your home computer, or a computer at school or the library, will give you a good idea as to whether desktop publishing is for you. Play around with various graphic design and page layout

The Home Office

The technology and software is constantly changing for those trying to stay ahead in the business of desktop publishing. But here are some basics of the home office:

- Computer (with CD-ROM/DVD-ROM drive and Internet hardware and software)
- Laser printer
- Scanner
- Page layout and design programs
- Word processing program
- Image editing software
- Illustration software
- Spreadsheet and database programs

programs. If you subscribe to an Internet service, take advantage of any free Web space available to you and design your own home page. Join computer clubs and volunteer to produce newsletters and flyers for school or community clubs. Volunteering is an excellent way to try new software and techniques as well as gain experience troubleshooting and creating final products. Part-time or summer employment with printing shops and companies that have in-house publishing or printing departments are other great ways to gain experience and make valuable contacts.

EMPLOYERS

Approximately 34,000 desktop publishing specialists are employed in the United States. Desktop publishing specialists work for individuals and small business owners, such as publishing houses, advertising agencies, graphic design agencies, and printing shops. Some large companies also contract with desktop publishing services rather than hire full-time designers. Government agencies such as the U.S. Government Printing Office hire desktop publishing specialists to help produce the large number of documents they publish.

Desktop publishing specialists deal directly with their clients, but in some cases they may be subcontracting work from printers, designers, and other desktop publishing specialists. They may also work as consultants, working with printing professionals to help solve particular design problems.

STARTING OUT

To start your own business, you must have a great deal of experience with design and page layout, and a careful understanding of the computer design programs you'll be using. Before striking out on your own, you may want to gain experience as a full-time staff member of a large business. Most desktop publishing specialists enter the field through the production side, or the editorial side of the industry. Those with training as a designer or artist can easily master the finer techniques of production. Printing houses and design agencies are places to check for production artist opportunities. Publishing companies often hire desktop publishing specialists to work in-house or as freelance employees. Working within the industry, you can make connections and build up a clientele.

You can also start out by investing in computer hardware and software, and volunteering your services. By designing logos, letterhead, and restaurant menus, for example, your work will gain quick recognition, and word of your services will spread.

ADVANCEMENT

The growth of Darryl and Maree Gabriel's business requires that they invest in another computer and printer. "We want to expand," Darryl says, "and develop with technology by venturing into Internet marketing and development. We also intend to be a thorn in the side of the larger commercial printing businesses in town."

In addition to taking on more print projects, desktop publishing specialists can expand their business into Web design and page layout for Internet-based magazines.

EARNINGS

There is limited salary information available for desktop publishing specialists, most likely because the job duties of desktop publishing specialists can vary and often overlap with other jobs. The average wage of desktop publishing specialists in the prepress department generally ranges from $15 to $50 an hour. Entry-level desktop publishing specialists with little or no experience generally earn minimum wage. Freelancers can earn from $15 to $100 an hour.

According to the U.S. Department of Labor, median annual earnings of desktop publishing specialists were $32,800 in 2005. The lowest 10 percent earned less than $19,190 and the highest 10 percent earned more than $53,750. Wage rates vary depending on experience, training, region, and size of the company.

WORK ENVIRONMENT

Desktop publishing specialists spend most of their time working in front of a computer, whether editing text, or laying out pages. They need to be able to work with other prepress professionals, and deal with clients. Hours may vary depending on project deadlines at hand. Some projects may take just a day to complete, while others may take weeks or months. Projects range from designing a logo for letterhead, to preparing a catalog for the printer, to working on a file for a company's Web site.

OUTLOOK

According to the U.S. Department of Labor, employment for desktop publishing specialists is projected to grow faster than the average occupation through 2014, even though overall employment in the printing industry is expected to decline slightly. This is due in part because electronic processes are replacing the manual processes

Learn More About It

Adobe Creative Team. *Adobe Illustrator CS2 Classroom in a Book* (w/ CD-Rom). San Jose, Calif.: Adobe Press, 2005.
Adobe Creative Team. *Adobe Photoshop CS2 Classroom in a Book* (w/ CD-ROM). San Jose, Calif.: Adobe Press, 2005.
Fanson, Barbara A. *Start and Run a Profitable Desktop Publishing Business.* 2d ed. North Vancouver, B.C.: Self-Counsel Press, 2004.
Kursmark, Louise. *How to Start a Home-Based Desktop Publishing Business.* 3d ed. Guilford, Conn.: Globe Pequot Press, 2002.
Lumgair, Christopher. *Teach Yourself Desktop Publishing.* New York: McGraw-Hill, 2003.
Parker, Roger C. *Looking Good in Print.* 6th ed. Scottsdale, Ariz.: Paraglyph Press, 2006.
Shaw, Lisa. *How to Make Money Publishing from Home.* 2d ed. Rocklin, Calif.: Prima Publishing, 2000.

performed by paste-up workers, photoengravers, camera operators, film strippers, and platemakers.

As technology advances, the ability to create and publish documents will become easier and faster, thus influencing more businesses to produce printed materials. Desktop publishing specialists will be needed to satisfy typesetting, page layout, design, and editorial demands. With new equipment, commercial printing shops will be able to shorten the turnaround time on projects and in turn can increase business and accept more jobs. For instance, digital printing presses allow printing shops to print directly to the digital press rather than printing to a piece of film, and then printing from the film to the press. Digital printing presses eliminate an entire step and should appeal to companies who need jobs completed quickly.

QuarkXPress, Adobe PageMaker, InDesign, Macromedia Free-Hand, Adobe Illustrator, and Adobe Photoshop are some programs often used in desktop publishing. Specialists with experience in these and other software will be in demand.

FOR MORE INFORMATION

This organization is a source of financial support for education and research projects designed to promote careers in graphic communications. For more information, contact
Graphic Arts Education and Research Foundation
1899 Preston White Drive

Reston, VA 20191-5468
Tel: 866-381-9839
Email: gaerf@npes.org
http://www.gaerf.org

For industry information, contact the following organizations:
Graphic Arts Information Network
200 Deer Run Road
Sewickley, PA 15143-2324
Tel: 412-741-6860
Email: gain@piagatf.org
http://www.gain.net

National Association for Printing Leadership
75 West Century Road
Paramus, NJ 07652-1408
Tel: 800-642-6275
Email: information@napl.org
http://www.recouncil.org

For information on careers, student competitions, and colleges that offer training in technical communication, contact
Society for Technical Communication
901 North Stuart Street, Suite 904
Arlington, VA 22203-1822
Tel: 703-522-4114
Email: stc@stc.org
http://www.stc.org

Visit the following Web site for information on scholarships, competitions, colleges and universities that offer graphic communication programs, and careers.
GRAPHIC COMM Central
Email: gcc@teched.vt.edu
http://teched.vt.edu/gcc

Editors

QUICK FACTS

School Subjects
English
Journalism

Personal Interests
Communication/ideas
Helping/teaching

Work Environment
Primarily indoors
Primarily one location

Minimum Education Level
Bachelor's degree

Salary Range
$26,910 to $45,510 to
$85,230+

Certification or Licensing
None available

Outlook
About as fast as the average

DOT
132

GOE
01.02.01

NOC
5122

O*NET-SOC
27-3041.00

OVERVIEW

Editors perform a wide range of functions, but their primary responsibility is to ensure that text provided by writers is suitable in content, format, and style for the intended audiences. Readers are an editor's first priority. Among the employers of editors are book publishers, magazines, newspapers, newsletters, advertising agencies, radio stations, television stations, Internet sites, and corporations of all kinds. There are about 127,000 editors employed in the United States.

HISTORY

The history of book editing is tied closely to the history of the book and the history of the printing process. The 15th century invention of the printing press by German goldsmith Johannes Gutenberg and the introduction of movable type in the West revolutionized the craft of bookmaking. Books could now be mass-produced. It also became more feasible to make changes to copy before a book was put into production. Printing had been invented hundreds of years earlier in China, but books did not proliferate there as quickly as they did in the West, which saw millions of copies in print by 1500.

In the early days of publishing, authors worked directly with the printer, and the printer was often the publisher and seller of the author's work. Eventually, however, booksellers began to work directly with the authors and eventually took over the role of publisher. The publisher then became the middleman between author and printer.

The publisher worked closely with the author and sometimes acted as the editor. The word *editor*, in fact, derives from the Latin

word *edere* or *editum* and means supervising or directing the preparation of text. Eventually, specialists were hired to perform the
editing function. These editors, who were also called advisors or
literary advisors in the 19th century, became an integral part of the
publishing business.

The editor, also called the sponsor in some houses, sought out
the best authors, worked with them, and became their advocate in
the publishing house. Some editors became so important that their

Joe Zee, Editor in Chief of *Vitals Magazine,* is shown in his New York
City Office. *(Paul Hawthorne/Getty Images)*

very presence in a publishing house could determine the quality of authors published there. Some author-editor collaborations have become legendary. The field has grown through the 20th and 21st century, with computers greatly speeding up the editorial process.

THE JOB

Editors work for many kinds of publishers, publications, and corporations. Editors' titles vary widely, not only from one area of publishing to another but also within each area.

Although some editors write for the organizations that employ them, most editors work with material provided by writers. For this reason, one of the most important steps in the editing process is acquiring the work of writers. In the fields of book and journal publishing, that work is usually performed by *acquisitions editors,* who are often called *acquiring editors.* Acquisitions editors may either generate their own ideas or use ideas provided by their publishers or other staff members. If they begin with an idea, they look for writers who can create an effective book or article based on that idea. One benefit of that method is that such ideas are ones that the editors believe are likely to be commercially successful or intellectually successful or both. Often, however, editors use ideas that they receive from writers in the form of proposals.

In some cases, the acquisitions editor will receive a complete manuscript from an author instead of a proposal. Most of the time, however, the writer will submit a query letter that asks whether the editor is interested in a particular idea. If the editor believes that the idea has potential and is suitable for the publishing house, the editor will discuss the idea further with the writer. Unless the writer is well-known or is known and trusted by the editor, the editor usually asks the writer for a sample chapter or section. If the editor likes the sample chapter and believes that the author can complete an acceptable manuscript, the publishing house will enter into a contract with the writer. In some cases, the editor will prepare that contract; in others, the publisher or someone else will prepare the contract at the publishing house. The contract will specify when the manuscript is due, how much the author will be paid, how long the manuscript must be, and what will happen if the author cannot deliver a manuscript that the editor believes is suitable for publication, among other things.

After the contract has been signed, the writer will begin work. The acquisitions editor must keep track of the author's progress. Publishing budgets must be prepared in advance so that vendors can be paid and books can be advertised, so it is important that the manuscript be delivered by the due date. Some authors work well on their own and complete their work efficiently and effectively. In many cases, however, authors have problems. They may need advice from the editor regarding content, style, or organization of information. Often, the editor will want to see parts of the manuscript as they are completed. That way, any problems in the writer's work can be identified and solved as soon as possible.

Some typical problems are statements the writer makes that may leave the publisher open to charges of libel or plagiarism. If this problem arises, the editor will require the writer to revise the manuscript. If the writer uses materials that were created by other people (such as long quotations, tables, or artwork), it may be necessary to request permission to use those materials. If permission is required but is not given, the materials cannot be used. It is usually the author's job to obtain permission, but sometimes the editor performs that task. In any case, the editor must make sure that necessary permissions are obtained. When an acceptable manuscript has been delivered, the acquisition editor's job is usually complete.

Some publishing houses have editors who specialize in working with authors. These *developmental editors* do not acquire manuscripts. Instead, they make sure the author stays on schedule and does a good job of writing and organizing their material.

Once an acceptable manuscript has been delivered to the publishing house, it is turned over to a *copy editor*. This editor's job is to read the manuscript carefully and make sure that it is sufficiently well written, factually correct (sometimes this job is done by a researcher or fact-checker), grammatically correct, and appropriate in tone and style for its intended readers. Any errors or problems in a printed piece reflect badly not only on the author but also on the publishing house.

The copy editor must be an expert in the English language, have a keen eye for detail, and know how to identify problems. The editor will simply correct some kinds of errors, but in some cases—especially when the piece deals with specialized material—the editor may need to ask, or query, the author about certain points. An editor must never change something that he or she does not understand, since one of the worst errors an editor can make is to change something that is correct to something that is incorrect.

After the copy editor has edited the manuscript, it may be (but is not always) sent to the author for review. When the editor and author have agreed on the final copy, the editor or another specialist will use various kinds of coding to mark the manuscript for typesetting. The codes, which usually correlate to information provided by a graphic designer, tell the typesetter which typefaces to use, how large to make the type, what the layout of the finished pages will look like, and where illustrations or other visual materials will be placed on the pages, among other things.

After the manuscript has been typeset and turned into galley proofs, or typeset copy that has not been divided into pages, the galleys are usually sent to the author to be checked. If the author finds errors or requests that changes be made, the copy editor or the *production editor* will oversee the process, determining which changes will be made.

Managing the editorial staff is the job of the *managing editor,* who draws up budgets for projects, oversees schedules, assigns projects to other editors, and ensures that the editorial staff is working efficiently. The managing editor's boss is the *editor in chief, editorial director,* or *executive editor.* This editor works closely with the publisher, determining the kinds of materials the house will publish and ensuring that the editorial staff carries out the wishes of the publisher. The editor in chief and managing editor also work closely with the heads of other departments, such as marketing, sales, and production.

The basic functions performed by magazine and newspaper editors are much like those performed by book editors, but staff writers do a significant amount of the writing that appears in magazines and newspapers, or periodicals. Periodicals often use editors who specialize in specific areas, such as *city editors,* who oversee the work of reporters who specialize in local news, and department editors. *Department editors* specialize in areas such as business, fashion, sports, and features, to name only a few. These departments are determined by the interests of the audience that the periodical intends to reach. Like book houses, periodicals use copy editors, researchers, and fact checkers, but at small periodicals, one or a few editors may be responsible for tasks that would be performed by many people at a larger publication.

REQUIREMENTS
High School
Editors must be expert communicators, so you should excel in English if you wish to be an editor. You must learn to write extremely well, since you will be correcting and even rewriting the work of others. If elective classes in writing are available in your school, take them. Study journalism and take communications courses. Work as a writer or editor for the school paper. Take a photography class. Since virtually all editors use computers, take computer courses. You absolutely must learn to type. If you cannot type accurately

and rapidly, you will be at an extreme disadvantage. Don't forget, however, that a successful editor must have a wide range of knowledge. The more you know about many areas, the more likely you will be to do well as an editor. Don't hesitate to explore areas that you find interesting. Do everything you can to satisfy your intellectual curiosity. As far as most editors are concerned, there is no useless information.

Postsecondary Training

An editor must have a bachelor's degree, and advanced degrees are highly recommended for book editors and magazine editors. Most editors have degrees in English or journalism, but it is not unheard of for editors to major in one of the other liberal arts. If you know that you want to specialize in a field such as scientific editing, you may wish to major in the area of science of your choice while minoring in English, writing, or journalism. There are many opportunities for editors in technical fields, since most of those who go into editing are interested primarily in the liberal arts. Many colleges offer courses in book editing, magazine design, general editing, and writing. Some colleges, such as the University of Chicago and Stanford University, offer programs in publishing, and many magazines and newspapers offer internships to students. Take advantage of these opportunities. It is extremely important that you gain some practical experience while you are in school. Work on the school paper or find a part-time job with a newspaper or magazine. Don't hesitate to work for a publication in a noneditorial position. The more you know about the publishing business, the better off you will be.

Other Requirements

Good editors are fanatics for the written word. Their passion for good writing comes close to the point of obsession. They are analytical people who know how to think clearly and communicate what they are thinking. They read widely. They not only recognize good English when they see it but also know what makes it good. If they read something they don't understand, they analyze it until they do understand it. If they see a word they don't know, they look it up. When they are curious about something, they research the subject.

You must pay close attention to details to succeed as an editor. You must also be patient, since you may have to spend hours turning a few pages of near-gibberish into powerful, elegant English. If you are the kind of person who can't sit still, you probably will not succeed as an editor. To be a good editor, you must be a self-starter who is not afraid to make decisions. You must be good not only at identifying problems but also at solving them, so you must be creative. If you are both creative and a perfectionist, editing may be the line of work for you.

EXPLORING

One of the best ways to explore the field of editing is to work on a school newspaper or other publication. The experience you gain will definitely be helpful, even if your duties are not strictly editorial. Being involved in writing, reporting, typesetting, proofreading, printing, or any other task will help you to understand editing and how it relates to the entire field of publishing.

If you cannot work for the school paper, try to land a part-time job with a local newspaper or newsletter, or publish your own newsletter. You may try combining another interest with your interest in editing. For example, if you are interested in environmental issues, you might want to start a newsletter that deals with environmental problems and solutions in your community.

Another useful project is keeping a journal. In fact, any writing project will be helpful, since editing and writing are inextricably linked. Write something every day. Try to rework your writing until it is as good as you can make it. Try different kinds of writing, such as letters to the editor, short stories, poetry, essays, comedic prose, and plays.

The American Copy Editors Society offers a wide variety of resources for aspiring and professional copy editors at its Web site (http://www.copydesk.org). These include articles about copyediting, a discussion board, a sample copyediting test, and suggested books and Web sites. The society also offers membership to high school students who are taking journalism courses or working on a school or alternative publication.

EMPLOYERS

Approximately 127,000 editors are employed in the United States. One of the best things about the field of editing is that there are many kinds of opportunities for editors. The most obvious employers for editors are book publishers, magazines, and newspapers. There are many varieties of all three of these types of publishers. There are small and large publishers, general and specialized publishers, local and national publishers. If you have a strong interest in a particular field, you will undoubtedly find various publishers that specialize in it.

Businesses offer another excellent source of employment for editors. Almost all businesses of any size need writers and editors on a full-time or part-time basis. Corporations often publish newsletters for their employees or produce publications that promote their services or talk about how they do business. Large companies produce annual reports that must be written and edited. In addition, advertising is a major source of work for editors, proofreaders, and writers. Advertising agencies use editors, proofreaders, and quality-control people, as do typesetting and printing companies (in many cases, proofreaders edit as well as proofread). Keep in mind that somebody has to work on all the printed material you see every day, from books and magazines to menus and matchbooks.

STARTING OUT

There is tremendous competition for editorial jobs, so it is important for a beginner who wishes to break into the business to be as well prepared as possible. College students who have gained experience as interns, have worked for publications during the summers, or have attended special programs in publishing will be at an advantage. In addition, applicants for any editorial position must be extremely careful when preparing cover letters and resumes. Even a single error in spelling or usage will disqualify an applicant. Applicants for editorial or proofreading positions must also expect to take and pass tests that are designed to determine their language skills.

Many editors enter the field as editorial assistants or proofreaders. Some editorial assistants perform only clerical tasks, whereas others may also proofread or perform basic editorial tasks. Typically, an editorial assistant who performs well will be given the opportunity to take on more and more editorial duties. Proofreaders have the advantage of being able to look at the work of editors, so they can learn while they do their own work.

Good sources of information about job openings are school career services offices, classified ads in newspapers and trade journals, specialized publications such as *Publishers Weekly* (http://publishersweekly.com), and Internet sites. One way to proceed is to identify local publishers through the Yellow Pages. Many publishers have Web sites that list job openings, and large publishers often have telephone job lines that serve the same purpose.

ADVANCEMENT

In book houses, employees who start as *editorial assistants* or *proofreaders* and show promise generally become copy editors. After gaining skill in that position, they may be given a wider range of duties while retaining the same title. The next step may be a position as a *senior copy editor,* which involves overseeing the work of junior copy editors, or as a *project editor.* The project editor performs a wide variety of tasks, including copyediting, coordinating the work of in-house and freelance copy editors, and managing the schedule of a particular project. From this position, one may move up to become *assistant editor,* then *managing editor,* then *editor in chief.* These positions involve more management and decision making than is usually found in the positions described previously. The editor in chief works with the *publisher* to ensure that a suitable editorial policy is being followed, while the managing editor is responsible for all aspects of the editorial department. The *assistant editor* provides support to the managing editor. (It should be noted that job titles and responsibilities can vary from publishing house to publishing house.)

Newspaper editors generally begin working on the copy desk, where they progress from less significant stories and projects to major news and feature stories. A common route to advancement is for copy editors to be promoted to a particular department, where they may move up the ranks to management positions. An editor who has achieved success in a department may become a city editor, who is responsible for news, or a managing editor, who runs the entire editorial operation of a newspaper.

Magazine editors advance in much the same way that book editors do. After they become copy editors, they work their way up to become senior editors, managing editors, and editors in chief. In many cases, magazine editors advance by moving from a position on one magazine to the same position with a larger or more prestigious magazine. Such moves often bring significant increases in both pay and status.

EARNINGS

Although a small percentage of editors are paid extremely well, the average editor is not well paid. Competition for editing jobs is fierce, and there is no shortage of people who wish to enter the field. For that reason, companies that employ editors generally pay relatively low wages.

According to 2005 data from the U.S. Department of Labor, median annual earnings for editors were $45,510. The lowest-paid 10 percent earned less than $26,910 and the highest-paid 10 percent earned more than $85,230. In 2005, the mean annual earnings for editors employed by newspaper, book, and directory publishers were $51,030; by professional and similar organizations, $53,980; and by advertising and related services, $55,090.

Technical editors usually make more money than newspaper, magazine, or book editors. According to a 2005 salary survey conducted by the Society for Technical Communication, the average salary for technical writers and editors is $67,520.

WORK ENVIRONMENT

The environments in which editors work varies widely. For the most part, publishers of all kinds realize that a quiet atmosphere is conducive to work that requires tremendous concentration. It takes an unusual ability to focus to edit in a noisy place. Most editors work in private offices or cubicles. Book editors often work in quieter surroundings than do newspaper editors or quality-control people in advertising agencies, who sometimes work in rather loud and hectic situations.

Even in relatively quiet surroundings, however, editors often have many distractions. A project editor who is trying to do some copyediting or review the editing of others may, for example, have to deal with phone calls from authors, questions from junior editors, meetings with members of the editorial and production staff, and questions from freelancers, among many other distractions. In many cases, editors have computers that are exclusively for their own use, but in others, editors must share computers that are located in a common area.

Deadlines are an important issue for virtually all editors. Newspaper and magazine editors work in a much more pressurized atmosphere than book editors because they face daily or weekly deadlines, whereas book production usually takes place over several months.

In almost all cases, editors must work long hours during certain phases of the editing process. Some newspaper editors start work at 5:00 A.M., others work until 11:00 P.M. or even through the night. Feature editors, columnists, and editorial page editors usually can schedule their day in a more regular fashion, as can editors who work on weekly newspapers. Editors working on hard news, however, may receive an assignment that must be completed, even if work extends well into the next shift.

OUTLOOK

According to the *Occupational Outlook Handbook,* employment of editors will increase about as fast as the average occupation through 2014. Competition for those jobs will remain intense, since so many people want to enter the field. Book publishing will remain particularly competitive, since many people still view the field in a romantic

Learn More About It

Connolly, William G., and Allan M. Siegal. *The New York Times Manual of Style and Usage: The Official Style Guide Used by the Writers and Editors of the World's Most Authoritative Newspaper.* New York: Three Rivers Press, 2002.

Gibaldi, Joseph. *MLA Style Manual and Guide to Scholarly Publishing.* 2d ed. New York: Modern Language Association of America, 1998.

Gross, Gerald. *Editors on Editing: What Writers Need to Know About What Editors Do.* 3d rev. ed. New York: Grove Press, 1994.

Microsoft Corporation. *The Microsoft Manual of Style for Technical Publications.* 3d ed. Redmond, Wash.: Microsoft Press, 2003.

Rude, Carolyn D. *Technical Editing.* 4th ed. Reading, Mass.: Longman, 2005.

Shertzer, Margaret. *The Elements of Grammar.* Reading, Mass.: Longman, 1996.

Strunk, William Jr., and E. B. White. *The Elements of Style.* 4th ed. Boston: Allyn & Bacon, 2000.

University of Chicago. *The Chicago Manual of Style: The Essential Guide for Writers, Editors, and Publishers.* 15th ed. Chicago, Ill.: The University of Chicago Press, 2003.

---

light. Much of the expansion in publishing is expected to occur in small newspapers, radio stations, and television stations. In these organizations, pay is low even by the standards of the publishing business.

One of the major trends in publishing is specialization. More and more publishing ventures are targeting relatively narrow markets, which means that there are more opportunities for editors to combine their work and their personal interests. It is also true, however, that many of these specialty publications do not survive for long.

There will be increasing job opportunities for editors in Internet publishing as online publishing and services continue to grow. Advertising and public relations will also provide employment opportunities.

A fairly large number of positions—both full-time and freelance—become available when experienced editors leave the business for other fields. Many editors make this decision because they find that they can make more money in other businesses than they can as editors.

FOR MORE INFORMATION

The following organization's Web site is an excellent source of information about careers in editing. The ACES organizes educational seminars and maintains lists of internships.
American Copy Editors Society (ACES)
Three Healy Street
Huntington, NY 11743-5323
http://www.copydesk.org

The ASNE helps editors maintain the highest standards of quality, improve their craft, and better serve their communities. It preserves and promotes core journalistic values. Visit its Web site to read online publications such as Why Choose Journalism? *and* Preparing for a Career in Newspapers.
American Society of Newspaper Editors (ASNE)
11690B Sunrise Valley Drive
Reston, VA 20191-1409
Tel: 703-453-1122
Email: asne@asne.org
http://www.asne.org

This organization of book publishers offers an extensive Web site about the book business.
Association of American Publishers
71 Fifth Avenue, 2nd Floor
New York, NY 10003-3004
Tel: 212-255-0200
Email: info@bookjobs.org
http://www.publishers.org

This organization provides information about internships and about the newspaper business in general.
Dow Jones Newspaper Fund
PO Box 300
Princeton, NJ 08543-0300
Tel: 609-452-2820
Email: newsfund@wsj.dowjones.com
http://www.djnewspaperfund.dowjones.com/fund

The EFA is an organization for freelance writers and editors. Members receive a newsletter and a free listing in their directory.
Editorial Freelancers Association (EFA)
71 West 23rd Street, Suite 1910

New York, NY 10010-4181
Tel: 866-929-5400
Email: office@the-efa.org
http://www.the-efa.org

This organization is a good source of information on internships.
Magazine Publishers of America
810 Seventh Avenue, 24th Floor
New York, NY 10019-5873
Tel: 212-872-3700
Email: mpa@magazine.org
http://www.magazine.org

For information on careers, contact:
Society for Technical Communication
901 North Stuart Street, Suite 904
Arlington, VA 22203-1822
Tel: 703-522-4114
Email: stc@stc.org
http://www.stc.org

The Slot is a Web site founded and maintained by Bill Walsh, financial copy desk chief at The Washington Post. *Walsh's tips on proper word usage, grammar lessons, and style guides are both informative and funny.*
The Slot
http://www.theslot.com

INTERVIEW

Clifford Thompson edits Current Biography *for the H.W. Wilson Company in New York. He spoke with the editors of* Careers in Focus: Writing *about his professional experience and the field of editing in general.*

Q. What are the primary responsibilities of your position?
A. I am the editor of the H. W. Wilson Company's reference publication *Current Biography*, which appears 11 times per year; the magazine's approximately 200 yearly articles are updated in the fall for the *Current Biography Yearbook*. I also oversee the publication of Wilson's other biographical books, including *Current Biography International* and *World Authors*. I choose

the subjects covered in those publications and oversee a staff of 15 editors and staff writers.

Q. How have your educational and professional achievements prepared you to be an editor?

A. In terms of professional qualifications, the most important move I ever made was to take a course (after college) in copyediting. Copy editors are concerned not with content but with grammar and style. (Examples of style choices: donut or doughnut? Is *New York Times* in quotes or italicized?) I learned how to use copyediting symbols (for example, how to indicate on a page that a letter should be capitalized) and other essential rules. That allowed me to get freelance copyediting work, which in turn gave me the experience to land a full-time position as a copy editor. From there I moved to content editing.

Q. What do you find most rewarding about your job?

A. Editing is skilled labor of the mind. As with any skill, using it well is very satisfying. Editing is the art of helping writers say that they mean, as smoothly and succinctly as possible. To use a simple example: "I only go to church on Sundays" means something different from "I go to church only on Sundays"; as an editor, I should not allow the writer to make the first statement when he or she (probably) means to make the second.

Q. What are some of the challenges of being an editor?

A. The idea, as I've mentioned, is to help writers say what they mean. What I must guard against as an editor is helping writers to say what I mean, or to express what they mean in a way no native speaker ever would. A good editor asserts authority without being domineering. As an editor I should not make any change simply because I can, and I should also be able to explain any change if asked to do so.

Q. What are the most important professional qualities for editors?

A. Topping the list is: a sense for the subtleties of meaning that different words and punctuation bring to a sentence. How one acquires that sense—whether it is an innate quality or a skill developed through reading—is a matter of debate. I suspect the answer is 70 percent the former and 30 percent the latter.

Q. In your experience, what types of companies or organizations employ editors?

A. Three obvious answers are newspapers, magazines, and book companies. An important thing to know is that no one starts off as an editor. (Copy editors are exceptions.) At newspapers or magazines people start as reporters or staff writers. At book companies, they start as editorial assistants – basically, glorified secretaries. (I did that for two years.) A drawback to being a book editor is that the workday involves a lot of meetings; very little actual editing gets done. The Wilson Company, where I work, is an exception in that regard, which is one thing I like about it.

Q. How have changes in technology transformed the process of editing?

A. Spellcheckers are enormously helpful. You still need to be careful, though: if you type "levy" when you mean "levee," the spellchecker won't help you. In terms of fact-checking and research, the Internet has made things easier. But again, beware—use reputable Internet sources. The Web is rife with misinformation.

Q. What advice would you give students who are interested in becoming editors?

A. Read as much good writing as you can.

Food Writers and Editors

OVERVIEW

Food writers write about food and drink. They may report on food- or cooking-related events, interview chefs or other food/cooking personalities, review recipes or restaurants, or simply write about a specific food or product. With their writing, they may persuade the general public to choose certain goods, services, and personalities.

Food editors perform a wide range of functions, but their primary responsibility is to ensure that text provided by food writers is suitable in content, format, and style for the intended audiences.

Food writers and editors work for magazines, trade journals, newspapers, books, and radio and television broadcasts. They may also work as freelancers.

HISTORY

The skill of writing has existed for thousands of years; writing about food has probably existed just as long. Recipes have been found recorded on clay tablets from Mesopotamia dating back more than 3,800 years. One of the oldest surviving cookbooks, *De Re Coquinaria*, is a collection of recipes generally attributed to a Roman gourmet by the name of Marcus Apicius, who lived during the 1st century.

After many centuries of writing recipes and cookbooks, people moved on to writing about food, its preparation, and reviewing food-serving establishments. One of the first magazines in the United

QUICK FACTS

School Subjects
English
Journalism

Personal Skills
Communication/ideas
Helping/teaching

Work Environment
Primarily indoors
Primarily one location

Minimum Education Level
Bachelor's degree

Salary Range
$19,000 to $46,420 to $89,940+ (writers)
$26,910 to $45,510 to $85,230+ (editors)

Certification or Licensing
None available

Outlook
About as fast as the average

DOT
131, 132

GOE
01.01.01, 01.01.02

NOC
5121, 5122

O*NET-SOC
27-3041.00, 27-3043.00

Food History Online

Interested in the history of cuisine, cookbooks, and cooking? The following Web sites are among the many online resources available for food history and research:

http://www.foodtimeline.org

http://foodhistorynews.com

http://www.epicurean.com

http://www.recipelink.com/history.html

http://whatscookingamerica.net/History/HistoryIndex.htm

http://www.foodreference.com

http://digital.lib.msu.edu/projects/cookbooks/index.html

States dedicated solely to food and wine, *Gourmet*, was founded in 1941. *Gourmet* was also the first U.S. magazine to regularly publish restaurant reviews, something that is quite common now.

Today, there are many magazines devoted to food, and most newspapers have sections devoted to food, as well. Take a walk down the food/cookbook aisle at any bookstore and the sheer number of books and the variety of food topics covered may amaze you. Today, food writers and editors are busier than ever.

THE JOB

Food writers and editors deal with the written word, whether the completed work is the printed page, broadcast, or on a computer screen. They tend to write about or edit all things related to food and beverages, such as recipes, new food products, meal planning and preparation, grocery shopping, cooking utensils and related products, and establishments that serve food and beverages. The nature of their work is as varied as the materials they produce: magazines, newspapers, books, trade journals and other publications, advertisements, and scripts for radio and television broadcast. The one common factor is the subject: food.

Food writers need to be able to write very clearly and descriptively, since the reader will not be able to taste, touch, or smell the product they are writing about. Depending on whether or not pictures accompany the written word, the reader may not even be able to see it. Food writers use their writing skills to write about many different things. They might write a press release about a new food product to be distributed to food editors at numerous newspapers and magazines. They may write a story about seasonal fruits and vegetables for a local television news broadcast. They may write an article for a women's magazine about new cooking utensils that make meal preparation easier for amateur chefs. They may write a review about a new restaurant that just opened.

Food writers who work for newspapers or magazines generally write about all things related to food and beverages, such as recipes, new food products, meal planning and preparation, grocery shopping, cooking utensils and related products, and establishments that serve food and beverages. Some food writers also cover other subject areas, as well, especially if they work for a newspaper or a general interest magazine, as opposed to a magazine dedicated solely to food.

Perhaps the most infamous type of food writer is the *food/restaurant critic*. The critic needs to be objective and fair with any type of product or restaurant review. When dining at a restaurant, he or she also needs to be anonymous, which is not always easy. While dining, food/restaurant critics need to make accurate observations and try to write or record them without arousing the suspicion of the restaurant staff, lest they realize they are being reviewed.

Food editors need to be able to polish the work of a food writer into a finished article or book. They correct grammar, spelling, and style, and check all the facts, especially where recipes are concerned. They are responsible for making sure that the writing adheres to any pertinent style guidelines, and that the writing is appropriate for the intended audience. When working for a magazine or newspaper, food editors may also be responsible for planning the editorial content of an entire food section, which can range in size from as little as half of a page to a multiple-page spread. Their duties may include assigning stories to staff or freelance writers, as well as assigning photography or artwork assignments as needed, to accompany the articles and recipes.

Food writers and editors who work for publishing houses may work on tour or guidebooks, writing and editing restaurant reviews and stories about regional food specialties. Or they may work with recipes and cookbooks, meticulously checking to ensure all ingredients and measurements are correct, and that no steps have been omitted from the cooking directions.

Food writers and editors can be employed either as in-house staff or as freelancers. Freelancers must provide their own office space and equipment, such as computers and fax machines. Freelance writers also are responsible for keeping tax records, sending out invoices, negotiating contracts, and providing their own health insurance.

REQUIREMENTS

High School

If you are interested in becoming a food writer or an editor, take English, general science, home economics, and computer classes while in high school. If they are offered at your school, take elective classes in writing or editing, such as journalism and business communications. Editors and writers in any areas must be expert communicators, so you should excel in English. You must learn to write well, since you will be correcting and even rewriting the work of others. While in high school, participating on the school's newspaper, yearbook, or any other publication will be of benefit to you.

Postsecondary Training

Most food writing and editing jobs require a college education. Some employers desire communications or journalism training in college. Others will require culinary coursework. Most schools offer courses in journalism and some have more specialized courses in book publishing, publication management, and newspaper and magazine writing.

Some employers require a degree or certificate from culinary school, or culinary work experience, in addition to a background in writing or editing. You may wish to take cooking classes from a local culinary school or community college to enhance your marketability as a food writer or editor.

In addition to formal course work, most employers look for practical writing and editing experience of any kind. Experience with college newspapers, yearbooks, or literary magazines will give you an edge, as well as if you have worked for small community newspapers or radio stations, even in an unpaid position. Many businesses, book publishers, magazines, newspapers, and radio and television stations have summer internship programs that provide valuable training. Interns do many simple tasks, such as run errands and answer phones, but some may be asked to perform research, conduct interviews, or even write or edit some minor pieces.

Other Requirements

In general, food writers and editors should be creative and able to express ideas clearly. Other assets include curiosity, persistence, initiative, resourcefulness, an accurate memory, and the ability to concentrate and produce quality work under pressure.

One last requirement, perhaps the most obvious, is that you should love food and everything to do with food. As a food writer or editor, you will spend much of your time sampling products, trying recipes, and writing or editing countless numbers of stories about food, so if you're not passionate about the subject, you will not be happy with your job.

EXPLORING

As a high school or college student, explore your interest in the fields of writing and editing by working as a reporter or writer on school newspapers, yearbooks, and literary magazines. If you cannot work for the school paper, try to land a part-time job on a local newspaper or newsletter. Explore your passion for food and increase your knowledge by taking cooking classes, attending ethnic festivals and food events, or touring different food-related businesses. Practice your own cooking, and always expand you knowledge about ingredients and preparation. Experiment with different types of restaurants and cuisines. After dining at a new restaurant, write about the experience. Review your writing. It is objective? Descriptive? Informative? Edit and rewrite it until you are satisfied with it.

Small community newspapers and local radio stations often welcome contributions from outside sources, although they may not be able to pay for them. Jobs in bookstores, magazine shops, and even newsstands offer a chance to become familiar with the various publications.

Professional organizations dedicated to food writing and editing, such as those listed at the end of this article, often provide information, resources, conferences, and other guidance programs that may be of interest to you.

EMPLOYERS

Food writers and editors work for a variety of employers. Magazines, newspapers, online publications, television and radio stations, book publishers, food/beverage manufacturing companies, and food/beverage trade associations all hire food writers and editors. Many food writers and editors work on a freelance basis, as well. Most employers are found in large cities such as New York, but virtually any geographical area served by a large newspaper will offer opportunities for a food writer or editor.

STARTING OUT

Most food writers and editors start out in entry-level positions. These jobs may be listed with college career services offices, or they may be obtained by applying directly to the employment departments of the individual newspapers, magazines, book publishers, or broadcasting companies. Graduates who previously had internships with these companies often have the advantage of knowing someone who can give them a personal recommendation or inform them of potential job openings before they are made public, thus giving them an edge over the competition. Want ads in newspapers and trade journals or on Web sites of professional associations are another source for jobs.

Some food writers and editors may start out writing and editing in a different subject area, and later choose to work with food when they have more seniority and priority in choosing work assignments. Other food writers and editors gain experience by freelancing, one article or review at a time. Even unpaid assignments can benefit the aspiring food writer or editor. They allow you to build up your portfolio of food-related writing and editing samples and provide you with contact with the people who may be in a position to hire you at a later time.

ADVANCEMENT

Food writers and editors are usually rewarded with higher profile assignments and increase in salary as they gain experience. For example, food writers may advance by moving from writing short filler copy or covering local events, to writing main features or traveling to cover high-profile industry events. In many cases, food writers and editors advance by moving from a position on one publication to the same position with a larger or more prestigious publication. Such moves may bring significant increases in both pay and status.

Sometimes freelance food writers and editors accept full-time positions with a newspaper or magazine. Such positions are usually offered on the merit of their previous freelance work for a publication. Other freelance food writers and editors may prefer to remain freelancers, but are able to command a higher paycheck because of their reputation and experience.

EARNINGS

In 2005, the median salary for writers, including food writers, was $46,420 a year, according to the U.S. Department of Labor (USDL). The lowest-paid 10 percent earned less than $24,320, while the highest-paid 10 percent earned $89,940 or more.

The USDL reports that the median annual salary for editors, including food editors, was $45,510 in 2005. The lowest paid 10 percent earned $26,910 or less, while the highest paid 10 percent earned $85,230 or more.

The International Association of Culinary Professionals (IACP) compiled a list of median salaries in 2002 for careers in the culinary field, including the following: cookbook author, $5,000 to $10,000 on their first book; cookbook editor, $27,000 to $85,000 annually; magazine food editor, $41,000 to $80,000 annually; newspaper food editor, $39,000 to $61,000 annually; food writer on staff at a publication, $19,000 to $40,000 annually; freelance food writer, $100 to $1,000 per story. In general, salaries are higher in large cities. Salaries are also dependent on the employer, as larger publications tend to pay more, and the writer or editor's level of experience, as those with many years of experience are able to earn a larger salary.

In addition to their salaries, many food writers and editors receive additional compensation. Most food critics, for example, have the meals they eat at a restaurant for the purpose of a review paid for by their employer. Some food writers and editors also receive travel expenses to cover expenditures such as mileage from driving to cover local events, or airfare and hotel accommodations for covering out-of-town industry events.

WORK ENVIRONMENT

Working conditions vary for food writers. Although the workweek usually runs 35 to 40 hours, many writers work during nontraditional hours or work overtime. Writers often work nights and weekends to cover food and beverage industry events, review restaurants, or to meet deadlines.

Many food writers work independently, but they often must cooperate with artists, photographers, editors, or advertising people who may have differing opinions of how the materials should be prepared and presented.

Physical surroundings range from comfortable private offices to noisy, crowded newsrooms filled with other workers typing and talking on the telephone. Food writers may be able to do much research via the library, Internet, or telephone interviews, but often may travel to local sites, other cities, or even out of the country.

The environments in which food editors work vary widely. Most editors work in private offices or cubicles. Book and magazine food editors often work in quieter surroundings than do newspaper food editors, who sometimes work in rather loud and hectic situations.

As with food writers, virtually all food editors must deal with the demands of deadlines. Newspaper and magazine food editors work in a much more pressurized atmosphere than book food editors because they face daily or weekly deadlines, whereas book production usually takes place over several months. In almost all cases, though, food editors must work long hours during certain phases of the editing process.

OUTLOOK

The employment of writers and editors, including food writers and editors, is expected to increase about as fast as the average rate of all occupations through 2014, according to the *Occupational Outlook Handbook*.

Individuals entering this field should realize that the competition for jobs is intense. Students just out of college may especially have difficulty finding employment. However, the subject of food and beverages continues to grow in popularity, thus providing more opportunities for those who wish to pursue a career in food writing and editing.

FOR MORE INFORMATION

The following organization is an excellent source of information about careers in copyediting. The ACES organizes educational seminars and maintains lists of internships.

American Copy Editors Society (ACES)
Three Healy Street
Huntington, NY 11743-5323
http://www.copydesk.org

The fund provides information about internships and about the newspaper business in general.

Dow Jones Newspaper Fund
PO Box 300
Princeton, NJ 08543-0300
Tel: 609-452-2820
Email: newsfund@wsj.dowjones.com
http://djnewspaperfund.dowjones.com/fund

The following is an organization for freelance writers and editors. Members receive a newsletter and a free listing in their directory.

Editorial Freelancers Association
71 West 23rd Street, Suite 1910
New York, NY 10010-4181
Tel: 866-929-5400
Email: office@the-efa.org
http://www.the-efa.org

This organization provides a wealth of industry information at its Web site.

International Association of Culinary Professionals
304 West Liberty Street, Suite 201
Louisville, KY 40202-3035

Tel: 502-581-9786
Email: iacp@hqtrs.com
http://www.iacp.com

This organization offers student membership, and an online news-letter and magazine at its Web site.
International Food, Wine & Travel Writers Association
1142 South Diamond Bar Boulevard, #177
Diamond Bar, CA 91765-2203
Tel: 877-439-8929
http://www.ifwtwa.org

The following organization is a good source of information about internships.
Magazine Publishers of America
810 Seventh Avenue, 24th Floor
New York, NY 10019-5873
Tel: 212-872-3700
Email: mpa@magazine.org
http://www.magazine.org

This organization offers student memberships for those interested in opinion writing.
National Conference of Editorial Writers
3899 North Front Street
Harrisburg, PA 17110-1583
Tel: 717-703-3015
Email: ncew@pa-news.org
http://www.ncew.org

The following organization's Web site provides information on issues facing food writers and editors, such as ethics, spelling guidelines, and criticism guidelines.
Association of Food Journalists (AFJ)
http://www.afjonline.com

This Web site offers online courses and a newsletter on writing about food.
Food Writing
Email: editor@food-writing.com
http://www.food-writing.com

Foreign Correspondents

QUICK FACTS

School Subjects
English
Foreign language
Journalism

Personal Skills
Communication/ideas
Helping/teaching

Work Environment
Indoors and outdoors
Primarily multiple locations

Minimum Education Level
Bachelor's degree

Salary Range
$18,300 to $32,270 to
$100,000+

Certification or Licensing
None available

Outlook
More slowly than the average

DOT
N/A

GOE
01.03.01

NOC
5123

O*NET-SOC
27-3022.00

OVERVIEW

Foreign correspondents report on news from countries outside of where their newspapers, radio or television networks, or wire services are located. They sometimes work for a particular newspaper, but since today's media focus more on local and national news, they usually rely on reports from newswire services to handle international news coverage rather than dispatching their own reporters to the scene. Only the biggest newspapers and television networks employ foreign correspondents. These reporters are usually stationed in a particular city and cover a wide territory.

HISTORY

James Gordon Bennett Sr., a prominent United States journalist and publisher of the *New York Herald*, was responsible for many firsts in the newspaper industry. He was the first publisher to sell papers through newsboys, the first to use illustrations for news stories, the first to publish stock-market prices and daily financial articles, and he was the first to employ European correspondents. Bennett's son, James Gordon Bennett Jr., carried on the family business and in 1871 sent correspondent Henry M. Stanley to central Africa to find Dr. David Livingstone, a famous British explorer who had disappeared.

In the early days, even magazines employed foreign correspondents. Famous American poet Ezra Pound, for example, reported from London for *Poetry* and *The Little Review*.

Rick Atkinson, foreign correspondent for *The Washington Post*, watches as a crowd gathers around a U.S. Army convoy in Karbala, Iraq. *(Associated Press)*

The inventions of the telegraph, telephone, typewriter, portable typewriter, the portable laptop computer, and the Internet all have contributed to the field of foreign correspondence.

THE JOB

The foreign correspondent is stationed in a foreign country where his or her job is to report on the news there. Foreign news can range from the violent (wars, coups, and refugee situations) to the calm (cultural events and financial issues). Although a domestic correspondent is responsible for covering specific areas of the news, like politics, health, sports, consumer affairs, business, or religion, foreign correspondents are responsible for all of these areas in the country where they are stationed. A China-based correspondent, for example, could spend a day covering the new trade policy between the United States and China, and the next day report on the religious persecution of Christians by the Chinese government.

A foreign correspondent often is responsible for more than one country. Depending on where he or she is stationed, the foreign correspondent might have to act as a one-person band in gathering and preparing stories.

"There are times when the phone rings at five in the morning and you're told to go to Pakistan," said Michael Lev, correspondent in Beijing, China, for the *Chicago Tribune*. "You must keep your wits about you and figure out what to do next."

For the most part, Lev decides on his own story ideas, choosing which ones interest him the most out of a myriad of possibilities. But foreign correspondents alone are responsible for getting the story done, and unlike reporters back home, they have little or no support staff to help them. Broadcast foreign correspondents, for example, may have to do their own audio editing after filming scenes. And just like other news reporters, foreign correspondents work under the pressure of deadlines. In addition, they often are thrown into unfamiliar situations in strange places.

Part of the importance of a foreign correspondent's job is keeping readers or viewers aware of the various cultures and practices held by the rest of the world. Michael Lev says he tries to focus on similarities and differences between the Asian countries he covers and the United States. "If you don't understand another culture, you are more likely to come into conflict with it," he says.

Foreign correspondents are drawn to conflicts of all kinds, especially war. They may choose to go to the front of a battle to get an accurate picture of what's happening. Or they may be able to get the story from a safer position. Sometimes they even face weapons trained directly on them.

Much of a foreign correspondent's time is spent doing research, investigating leads, setting up appointments, making travel arrangements, making on-site observations, and interviewing local people or those involved in the situation. The foreign correspondent often must be experienced in taking photographs or shooting video.

Living conditions can be rough or primitive, sometimes without running water. The job can sometimes be isolating.

After correspondents have interviewed sources and noted observations about an event or filmed it, they put their stories together, writing on computers and using modern technology like the Internet, e-mail, satellite telephones, and fax machines to finish the job and transmit the story to their newspaper, broadcast station, or wire service. Many times, correspondents work out of hotel rooms.

REQUIREMENTS

High School

In addition to English and creative writing needed for a career in journalism, you should study languages, social studies, political science, history, and geography. Initial experience may be gained by working on your school newspaper or yearbook, or taking advantage of study-abroad programs.

Postsecondary Training
In college, pursuing a journalism major is helpful but may not be crucial to obtaining a job as a foreign correspondent. Classes, or even a major, in history, political science, or literature could be beneficial. Studying economics and foreign languages also help.

Other Requirements
To be a foreign correspondent, in addition to a love of adventure, you need curiosity about how other people live, diplomacy when interviewing people, courage to sometimes confront people on uncomfortable topics, the ability to communicate well, and the discipline to sometimes act as your own boss. You also need to be strong enough to hold up under pressure yet flexible enough to adapt to other cultures.

EXPLORING
Does this type of work interest you? To explore this field, you can begin by honing your skills as a journalist. Join your high school newspaper staff to become a regular columnist or write special feature articles. Check out your high school's TV station and audition to be an anchor. Is there a radio station at your school? If so, volunteer to be on the staff there. And what about the Web? If your school has an online newspaper, get involved with that project. Gain as much experience as you can using different media to learn about the strengths and weaknesses of each and find out where you fit in best. You can also ask your high school journalism teacher or guidance counselor to help you set up an informational interview with a local journalist. Most are happy to speak with you when they know you are interested in their careers. It may be possible to get a part-time or summer job working at a local TV or radio station or at the newspaper office. Competition for one of these jobs, however, is strong because many college students take such positions as interns and do the work for little or no pay.

EMPLOYERS
Foreign correspondents work for newswire services, such as the Associated Press, Reuters, and Agence-France Press; major metropolitan newspapers; news magazines; and television and radio networks. These media are located in the largest cities in the United States and in the case of Reuters and Agence-France Press, in Europe.

STARTING OUT

College graduates have a couple of paths to choose between on their way to becoming a foreign correspondent. They can decide to experience what being a foreign correspondent is like immediately by going to another country, perhaps one whose language is familiar to them, and freelancing or working as a stringer. That means writing stories and offering them to anyone who will buy them. This method can be hard to accomplish financially in the short run but can pay off substantially in the long run.

Another path is to take the traditional route of a journalist and try to get hired upon graduation at any newspaper, radio station, or television station you can. It helps in this regard to have worked at a summer internship during your college years. Recent college graduates generally get hired at small newspapers or media stations, although a few major metropolitan dailies will employ top graduates for a year with no guarantee of their being kept on afterward. After building experience at a small paper or station, a reporter can try to find work at progressively bigger ones. Reporters who find employment at a major metropolitan daily that uses foreign correspondents can work their way through the ranks to become one. This is the path Michael Lev took, and he became a foreign correspondent when he was in his early 30s. He suggests that working for a wire service may allow a reporter to get abroad faster, but he thinks more freedom can be found working for a newspaper.

ADVANCEMENT

Foreign correspondents can advance to other locations that are more appealing to them or that offer a bigger challenge. Or they can return home to become columnists, editorial writers, editors, or network news directors.

EARNINGS

Salaries vary greatly depending on the publication, network, or station, and the cost of living and tax structure in various places around the world where foreign correspondents work. Generally, salaries range from $50,000 to an average of about $75,000 to a peak of $100,000 or more. Some media will pay for living expenses, such as the costs of a home, school for the reporter's children, and a car.

According to the U.S. Department of Labor, correspondents and other news reporters earned a median salary of $32,270 in 2005.

The lowest-paid 10 percent earned $18,300 or less, and the highest-paid 10 percent earned $71,220 or more.

WORK ENVIRONMENT

Correspondents and other reporters may face a hectic work environment since they often have tight deadlines and have to produce their reports with little time for preparation. Correspondents who work in countries that face great political or social problems risk their health and even their lives to report breaking news. Covering wars, political uprisings, fires, floods, and similar events can be extremely dangerous.

Working hours vary depending on the correspondent's deadlines. Their work often demands irregular or long hours. Because foreign correspondents report from international locations, this job involves frequent and long-term travel. The amount of travel depends on the size of the region the correspondent covers.

OUTLOOK

Although employment at newspapers, radio stations, and television stations in general is expected to grow more slowly than the average, the number of foreign correspondent jobs has leveled off. The employment outlook is expected to remain relatively stable, or even increase should a major conflict or war occur.

Factors that keep the number of foreign correspondents low are the high cost of maintaining a foreign news bureau and the relative lack of interest Americans show in world news. Despite these factors, the number of correspondents is not expected to decrease. There are simply too few as it is; decreasing the number could put the job in danger of disappearing, which most journalists believe is not an option. For now and the near future, most job openings will arise from the need to replace those correspondents who leave the job.

FOR MORE INFORMATION

The ASJA promotes the interests of freelance writers. It provides information on court rulings dealing with writing issues, has a writers' referral service, and offers a newsletter.
American Society of Journalists and Authors (ASJA)
1501 Broadway, Suite 302
New York, NY 10036-5505
Tel: 212-997-0947
http://www.asja.org

This association provides the annual publication Journalism and Mass Communication Directory *with information on educational programs in all areas of journalism (newspapers, magazines, television, and radio).*
Association for Education in Journalism and Mass Communication
234 Outlet Pointe Boulevard
Columbia, SC 29210-5667
Tel: 803-798-0271
http://www.aejmc.org

This organization's online Career Center has information on jobs, scholarships, internships, college programs, and other resources.
National Association of Broadcasters (NAB)
1771 N Street, NW
Washington, DC 20036-2800
Tel: 202-429-5300
Email: nab@nab.org
http://www.nab.org

The SPJ has chapters all over the United States. The SPJ's Web site offers information on careers, internships, and fellowships.
Society of Professional Journalists (SPJ)
Eugene S. Pulliam National Journalism Center
3909 North Meridian Street
Indianapolis, IN 46208-4011
Tel: 317-927-8000
http://www.spj.org

Visit the following Web site for comprehensive information on journalism careers, summer programs, and college journalism programs.
High School Journalism
http://www.highschooljournalism.org

Grant Coordinators and Writers

OVERVIEW

Grant coordinators are responsible for managing all grant-funded programs for nonprofit organizations. *Grant writers* handle the actual creation and preparation of proposals to potential funders. In smaller organizations, both jobs may be handled by the same person. Both grant coordinators and grant writers may work for schools, local governments, social service agencies, and other organizations to oversee all aspects of grant funding. The Association of Fundraising Professionals reports that it has nearly 28,000 members employed at a variety of nonprofit organizations, including those in the arts, social service, health care, and educational fields, as well as at private consulting firms around the country.

HISTORY

The first recorded government research grant was given to the inventor Samuel Morse in 1842. In the United States, the amount of grant-based funding has grown consistently and dramatically since that time. More private foundations began bestowing grants when it became clear how much help they could provide to all types of nonprofit groups. Government agencies have increased grants funding, especially in the sciences, recognizing that these grants help U.S. scientists and inventors stay on the cutting edge of new technology.

It is only in the last few decades that the positions of grant coordinator and grant writer have come into being. Organizing and writing grant proposals was usually assigned to various employees (who had other job duties) in each nonprofit agency. Now more and more

QUICK FACTS

School Subjects
Business
English

Personal Skills
Communication/ideas
Leadership/management

Work Environment
Primarily indoors
Primarily one location

Minimum Education Level
Bachelor's degree

Salary Range
$39,000 to $65,571 to $100,000

Certification or Licensing
Voluntary

Outlook
About as fast as the average

DOT
169

GOE
N/A

NOC
N/A

O*NET-SOC
N/A

Philanthropic Giving

More than $260 billion were given to a wide variety of organizations in 2005. The following table offers a breakdown of contributors.

Contributor	Amount Given	Percent of Total
Individuals	$199.07 billion	76.5
Foundations	$30.00 billion	11.5
Bequests	$17.44 billion	6.7
Corporations	$13.77 billion	5.3

Source: AAFRC Trust for Philanthropy/Giving USA 2006

agencies are recognizing the value of having separate grant coordinators and writers who work solely on grants for the agency.

THE JOB

The number of grants awarded each year in the United States is very large, and so is the competition among grants seekers; hundreds of institutions may apply for the same grant. Furthermore, organizations that award grants have very specific rules and requirements that must be satisfied for a proposal even to be considered.

Grant coordinators must be familiar with all applicable funding organizations and their requirements. They often make the difference in securing the grant for their organizations. Grant coordinators plan and organize all grant-funded programs for their agency or organization. They conduct extensive research on foundations and grant-offering agencies by ordering their publications and contacting officials at the foundations.

To determine which grants the organization should apply for, coordinators work with other officers in their own agency. Grant coordinators participate in many of the planning stages for the agency. For instance, they may sit in on meetings in which budgets are planned and financial officials determine operating budgets, anticipate income, and forecast expenditures. Employees of the non-profit organization may suggest programs, equipment, or materials that they would like to have funded by a grant, and the grant coordinator determines the best sources of funding for each need.

Before applying for a grant, a grant coordinator maps out a proposal for how the funding would be used. Often these proposals are long and complex. Other employees may help the grant coordinator write up a proposal justifying the need for the program or equipment.

Some nonprofit organizations are fortunate enough to have one or more employees whose primary function is grant writing. In these cases the grant coordinator does not write the grant proposal. The grant writer creates the proposal document, developing its vocabulary and overall structure. Working with the staff whose programs require funding, the grant writer devises a strategy, translating the program to make it relevant to the funder's interests. In the proposal, the grant writer also must communicate both the short-term and long-term goals of the organization so that they are understandable to an outsider. The grant writer also may be responsible for assembling supporting documents that accompany the proposal, such as the organization's budget, board of directors, history, mission, and executive biographies. The grant writer must create different proposals for different kinds of funding, for example, general operating support for the organization overall versus funding for a specific program or project. Additionally, if a grant is received, the grant writer often has to prepare a final report required by many funders.

When an organization does not have a separate grant writer on staff, the writer may be a financial officer in the organization, a teacher in the school, or an employee in charge of a particular project.

Drafts of the proposal usually pass through many hands, including fiscal officers or other executives, before being sent to foundations or grant-offering agencies. Once a final draft has been approved, the grant coordinator or writer prepares the grant proposal using the format required by the funding agency. The proposal then is submitted to the foundation or funding agency. It is the responsibility of the grant coordinator or writer to follow up on the application and meet with agency or foundation representatives if necessary.

Once an organization receives its grant, the coordinator makes sure to meet all of the requirements of the grant-giver. For example, if the grant covers the purchase of equipment, the coordinator confirms receipt of the correct equipment and completes follow-up reports for the foundation or agency. In some instances, the grant coordinator hires an outside agency to monitor the implementation of a grant-funded program. The outside agency then may submit its periodic monitoring reports both to the funding agency and to the grant coordinator.

A large part of the grant coordinator's work involves maintaining files and overseeing paperwork, which is usually done on computer. A thorough grant coordinator must keep the literature published by funding agencies for reference and file copies of all applications and proposals.

Grant coordinators are essentially project managers. They must understand the overall work of their organization while focusing on finding and obtaining the best grants. They see to it that their organization presents itself to funding agencies in the best possible way.

REQUIREMENTS

High School

High school courses in English, journalism, and creative writing, will help you develop your written communication skills. Courses in history and the humanities in general also are useful as background reference, and a solid background in mathematics will help you feel comfortable dealing with budgets and other financial documents.

Postsecondary Training

A 2004 survey by the Association of Fundraising Professionals reports that 95.4 percent of respondents held a college degree; of this group, 42 percent held a master's degree or higher. Grant coordinators and writers can have any of several kinds of educational backgrounds. Some study liberal arts, some have business degrees, and some have studied in management training programs.

Regardless of your educational background, you will need the ability to communicate clearly and effectively in writing. Much paperwork is involved in applying for a grant; the funding agency's instructions must be followed precisely, and the proposal must state the institution's goals and objectives in a clear and persuasive way.

Certification or Licensing

The American Grant Writers Association awards the certified grant writer designation to applicants who complete a four-day, 25-hour workshop. This workshop is designed for grant writers who are employed by nonprofit organizations, religious organizations, schools, and government agencies. Contact the association for more information.

The Association of Fundraising Professionals offers the certified fund raising executive designation to professionals who have at least five years experience in the field, fill out an application, pass a written examination, and pledge to uphold a code of ethics. This voluntary certification must be renewed every three years. The certification program is administered by CFRE International. Contact the organization for more information.

There is no licensing requirement or specific test that grant coordinators or writers must pass to work in the field.

Other Requirements

Most grant coordinators learn their work on the job. Experience in the workplace helps the coordinator locate the best sources of grants funding and learn the best ways to pursue those sources. For example, if the ideals of a foundation match the intent of the grant coordinator's agency, an ongoing relationship may develop between the agency and the foundation. The grant coordinator learns about these connections in the day-to-day work.

Grant coordinators must have good administrative skills and be detail-oriented. Good communication skills are essential. They work with a wide range of people and must express themselves easily. Coordinators direct and supervise others, so they must be comfortable in management situations. They should be able to influence and persuade others, including their associates and foundation employees. The more grant coordinators and writers understand about the operations of the foundations that they will be applying to, the more successful they will be in writing the grant proposals and securing the requested funding. Grant coordinators and writers must also work well under pressure. There are deadlines to meet, and the responsibility for meeting those deadlines falls squarely on their shoulders. The financial pressure on an organization that does not receive an expected grant can be enormous, and the grant coordinator may bear the responsibility for the loss.

EXPLORING

Volunteering for nonprofit organizations is a good way to find out about a grant coordinator's work firsthand. Contact local churches or synagogues, charities, health organizations, or social service agencies. In nonprofit organizations that have grant coordinators, the ideal internship or volunteer experience involves assisting with a grant application project. Sometimes schools have their own grant application projects several times a year. You can get an understanding of all of the work involved by seeing the application or proposal process through from start to finish.

Several organizations sponsor intensive workshops on grant coordination and fund-raising. The Grantsmanship Center (http://www.tgci.com) conducts seminars and workshops in cities across the United States 150 times a year. It helps grant coordinators and writers with proposal writing and other aspects of their jobs. Its

Who Receives Charitable Contributions?

The following table shows the wide variety of organizations that received more than $260 billion that was donated in 2005.

Recipient	Amount Received	Percent of Total
Religious	$93.18 billion	35.8
Education	$38.56 billion	14.8
Human Services	$25.36 million	9.7
Health	$22.54 billion	8.7
Foundations	$21.7 billion	8.3
Unallocated Giving	$16.5 billion	6.2
Public-society benefit	$14.03 billion	5.4
Arts, culture, and humanities	$13.51 billion	5.2
Environment/Animals	$8.86 billion	3.4
International Affairs	$6.39 billion	2.5

Source: AAFRC Trust for Philanthropy/Giving USA 2006

publication, *The Grantsmanship Center Magazine*, and the guide, *Program Planning and Proposal Writing*, are good resources for grant writers and coordinators. The Grantsmanship Center also maintains a reference library. The National Network of Grantmakers (http://www.nng.org) also offers seminars and publications.

Many fund-raising organizations also have helpful publications for the potential grant coordinator. An annual almanac, *Giving USA* is published by the Giving Institute: Leading Consultants to Non-Profits (http://www.aafrc.com).

Some colleges and universities offer courses in fund-raising. These may even include business lectures or seminars on the grant application process. Many colleges also offer courses in arts management or in nonprofit work that would help potential grant coordinators and writers understand the type of work required in this occupation.

EMPLOYERS

Grant writers and coordinators work for nonprofit organizations and agencies, such as social service agencies, arts organizations, museums, educational institutions, and research foundations. Grant writers also work independently as freelancers. They contract their services to smaller nonprofit agencies or individuals who might seek funding for an arts program or a scientific research project, for example.

STARTING OUT

After earning your bachelor's degree, apply for a job at a nonprofit organization. Keep in mind that you will probably be hired by an agency to do tasks other than grant writing or coordinating. You first need to learn how the organization operates and understand its goals before beginning to work with grants. In these first years, many prospective coordinators and writers sign up for management training programs or courses in technical writing, psychology, sociology, and statistical methods.

ADVANCEMENT

Since grant coordinators almost always begin their careers in other work, they advance into grant positions by showing an understanding of the organization's goals. Once the organization moves a person into a grant position, advancement comes with successful work on grant proposals and obtaining the necessary funding. If the grant coordinator and writer positions are separate, usually grant writers advance to grant coordinators, having gained expertise and familiarity with the funding community. But because nonprofit organizations often employ only one person responsible for grant writing and coordination, a grant administrator often advances by moving into a position with a larger nonprofit organization that requires higher-level skills.

EARNINGS

According to the *Compensation in Nonprofit Organizations 2005* report, grant writers had median incomes of $39,000 in 2005. The average salaries of surveyed members of the Association of Fundraising Professionals were much higher, at $65,751 a year in 2004. The salary survey noted that earnings varied among members based on position, organization, location, and experience. Pay differences based on gender and ethnic background were also discovered.

Freelance grant coordinators usually charge separate fees for research and grant writing.

Benefits for grant coordinators and writers often are equivalent to other professional business positions, including paid vacation, group insurance plans, and paid sick days.

WORK ENVIRONMENT

Grant coordinators work primarily in comfortable office environments. Some nonprofit agencies have cramped or inadequate facilities, while others may be quite luxurious. The grant coordinator usually works during regular office hours unless a deadline must be met. When grant coordinators approach the deadlines for submitting grant proposals, overtime work, including nights or weekends, may be required. Meetings with foundation representatives may take place outside the office or before or after regular hours. Benefits packages and vacation time vary widely from agency to agency, but most nonprofit organizations are flexible places to work. Grant coordinators are often most satisfied with their jobs when they believe in the goals of their own agency and know they are helping the agency do its work.

OUTLOOK

The outlook for grant coordinators and writers is steady. Although overall giving has increased over the last several years, hundreds of agencies are applying for the same grants—which has resulted in strong competition for funding. A top grant coordinator or writer can make the difference between the organization that gets funding and one that does not. A grant coordinator who has proven success in coordinating grants proposals and obtaining grants, as well as a grant writer who has written successful proposals, should be able to find work. Many people who work in nonprofit organizations believe that more grant coordinators and writers will be hired as more of these organizations realize that a professional grant administrator may help them get funding they have been missing. The grant coordinator's knowledge of how to choose the most appropriate sources of grant funding and implement funding programs is invaluable to nonprofit organizations.

FOR MORE INFORMATION

For information on certification, contact
American Grant Writers' Association
PO Box 8481
Seminole, FL 33775-8481
Tel: 727-366-9334
Email: customerservice@agwa.us
http://www.agwa.us

For information on fund-raising careers, educational programs, and other resources, contact
Association of Fundraising Professionals
4300 Wilson Boulevard, Suite 300
Arlington, VA 22203-4168
Tel: 703-684-0410
http://www.afpnet.org

For information on certification as a certified fundraising executive, contact:
CFRE International
4900 Seminary Road, Suite 670
Alexandria, VA 22311-1811
Tel: 703-820-5555
Email: info@cfre.org
http://www.cfre.org

This organization is a coalition of consulting firms working in the nonprofit sector.
Giving Institute: Leading Consultants to Non-Profits
4700 West Lake Avenue
Glenview, IL 60025-1468
Tel: 800-462-2372
Email: info@givinginstitute.org
http://www.aafrc.org

The following organization provides assistance on proposal writing, offers 200 seminars annually, and publishes The Grantsmanship Center Magazine.
Grantsmanship Center
PO Box 17220
Los Angeles, CA 90017-0220
Tel: 213-482-9860
Email: tgci@tgci.com
http://www.tgci.com

Greeting Card Designers and Writers

QUICK FACTS

School Subjects
Art
Computer science
English

Personal Skills
Artistic
Communication/ideas

Work Environment
Primarily indoors
Primarily one location

Minimum Education Level
High school diploma

Salary Range
$23,160 to $38,390 to
$67,660+ (designers)
$24,320 to $46,420 to
$89,940+ (writers)

Certification or Licensing
None available

Outlook
About as fast as the average

DOT
142 (designers)
132 (writers)

GOE
01.04.02 (designers)
01.02.01 (writers)

NOC
5241 (designers)
5121 (writers)

O*NET-SOC
27-1024.00 (designers)
27-3043.02 (writers)

OVERVIEW

Greeting card designers and writers either work as freelancers or as staff members of greeting card and gift manufacturers. Designers use artistic skills to create illustrated or photographic images for cards, posters, mugs, and other items generally sold in card shops; writers compose the expressions, poems, and jokes that accompany the images. The Greeting Card Association estimates that there are approximately 3,000 large and small greeting card publishers in America.

HISTORY

The Valentine is considered by many to be the earliest form of greeting card. Up until the fifth century, Romans celebrated a fertility festival called Lupercalia every February 15. At the feast, women wrote love notes and dropped them in an urn; the men would pick a note from the urn, then seek the company of the woman who composed the note. But the mass-produced holiday cards we know today didn't originate until the 1880s in England and America. With low printing costs and postage rates, the colorful, cheerful, and beautifully illustrated cards of the day quickly grew in popularity.

THE JOB

From sincere statements of love to jocular jabs, the contemporary greeting card industry provides a note for practically every expression. Hallmark and American Greetings are the biggest names in the business, offering cards for many occasions. Other card companies have carved out their own individual niches, like C-Ya, which sells "relationship closure cards" to send to ex-boyfriends and ex-girlfriends, former bosses, and anybody you don't ever want to see again. Though some of these companies use the talents of full-time staff writers and designers, others rely on freelancers to submit ideas, images, and expressions. In addition to greeting card production, some companies buy words and images for e-mail greetings, and for lines of products like mugs, posters, pillows, and balloons.

Bonnie Neubauer, a freelance writer in Pennsylvania, has tapped into the business-to-business greeting card niche. "[These cards] are tools to help sales people," Neubauer explains. "They help business people keep in touch." She sells her ideas to a small company called IntroKnocks Business Greetings. Many other greeting card companies are getting into business-to-business cards, such as Hallmark. "So many people communicate through faxes, e-mails, and voice mail," Neubauer says, "that when a card comes in a colored envelope, with a handwritten address, it gets attention."

To spark ideas, Neubauer reads industry trade magazines, visits company Web sites, and looks over books of stock photos. Once she recognizes a business need, she comes up with a card to meet the need. "Some people only send out cartoons," she says about the business-to-business greeting card marketplace, "while others are more serious and only want cards with sophisticated photographs."

Working from home offices, greeting card writers and designers come up with their ideas, then submit them to the companies for consideration. "Coming up with good card ideas," Neubauer says, "involves taking cliches, and combining them with a tad of humor." Artists and photographers submit reproductions of their work, rather than their originals, because some companies don't return unaccepted submissions or may lose the submissions in the review process. Artists submit prints, color copies, duplicate transparencies, or digital files. Writers submit their ideas on index cards or by e-mail.

REQUIREMENTS

High School

Hone your writing and artistic skills in high school by taking English and art classes. Since many designers use computers to create their designs, computer science courses also will be helpful.

Top Card-Sending Holidays

According to the Greeting Card Association, the top five card-sending holidays are:

Christmas	60 percent
Valentine's Day	25 percent
Mother's Day	4 percent
Easter	3 percent
Father's Day	3 percent

At the bottom of the holiday list? National Bosses Day.

Postsecondary Training

College education is not necessary for freelancing as an artist and writer, though card companies looking to hire you for a full-time staff position may require a background in English, creative writing, graphic design, or commercial arts. Even if you only want to freelance, community college courses that instruct you in the use of computer design programs can help you to create professional-looking images for submission to companies.

Certification or Licensing

No certification program exists for greeting card writers or designers. However, if you decide to print your own cards and sell them to stores and representatives, you may be required by your state to maintain a business license.

Other Requirements

"I'm extremely self-motivated and grossly optimistic," Bonnie Neubauer says, in regard to making her home business a success. As for the writing itself, Neubauer emphasizes the importance of a sense of humor. "I love word-play," she says, "and I love marketing and promotions." Any writer and designer should also be patient, persistent, and capable of accepting rejection.

EXPLORING

Try writing and designing your own greeting cards. There are many software programs that will help you create attractive cards, stationery, and newsletters. Ask your high school English teacher or counselor to set up an interview with a greeting card designer or freelance writer.

EMPLOYERS

As a freelancer, you can work anywhere in the country and submit your work through the mail. *Artist & Graphic Designers Market* and *Writer's Market,* reference books published annually by Writer's Digest (http://www.writersdigest.com), include sections listing the greeting card companies that accept submissions from freelance artists and writers. While some companies only buy a few ideas a year, others buy hundreds of ideas. Hallmark, by far the largest greeting card manufacturer, doesn't accept unsolicited ideas, but hires many creative people for full-time staff positions. However, because of Hallmark's reputation as a great employer, competition for those positions is high.

STARTING OUT

Get to know the market by visiting local card shops; find out what's popular, and what kinds of cards each company sells. Visit the Web sites of the greeting card companies listed in *Artist & Graphic Designers Market* and *Writer's Market* and study their online catalogs. Most companies have very specific guidelines; one may publish only humorous cards, while another may only publish inspirational poems. Once you have a good sense of what companies are looking for, contact manufacturers, find out their submission guidelines, and send in samples of your work.

Another opportunity to break into the industry is through an internship. Every year, Hallmark holds a competition for their writing and editing internships. (See their contact information at the end of this article.)

ADVANCEMENT

After you have submitted a lot of your work to many different companies, you will begin to make connections with people in the business. These connections can be valuable, leading you to jobs with better pay (such as royalties and percentages) and exclusive contracts. As you get to know the business better, you may choose to produce and market your own line of cards.

EARNINGS

Salaries vary widely among freelance greeting card writers and designers. Some card designers and writers sell only a few ideas a year. Others make a great deal of money, working exclusively with a company, or by manufacturing and distributing their own lines of cards and products. Card companies typically pay freelancers fees for each idea they buy. Some manufacturers may offer a royalty payment plan, including an initial advance. A small company may pay as little as $15 for an idea, while a larger company may pay $150 or more.

According to the U.S. Department of Labor, graphic designers earned a median annual salary of $38,190 in 2005, but pay ranged from less than $23,160 to more than $67,660. Writers of all types earned a median salary of $46,420 in 2005. The lowest-paid 10 percent earned less than $24,320 while the highest-paid writers earned more than $89,940 a year.

WORK ENVIRONMENT

Both writers and designers spend most of their time in an office, whether at home or in a company's space. Much of their work is done on a computer, whether they are designing images or writing copy. However, coming up with the initial ideas may involve a more creative routine. Many artists have certain activities that inspire them, such as listening to music, looking at photography and art books, or reading a novel.

OUTLOOK

According to the Greeting Card Association (GCA), the greeting card industry's retail sales have increased steadily from $2.1 billion in 1980, to more than $7.5 billion today. From designing animated e-mail messages to greeting card CD-ROM programs, greeting card writers and designers will likely find more and more outlets for their work. Advances in Web technology should also aid the card designer in posting his or her ideas and images online to invite companies to browse, download, and purchase ideas.

Average growth is expected for this career in coming years. Despite the growing popularity of e-mail, GCA says the industry will not be adversely affected. E-cards are not as personal as standard greeting cards, nor are they appropriate for many situations, such as weddings, anniversaries, or for expressing sympathy. "Just as the VCR has not been the death of the movie house, so too the Internet will not be the death knell of the paper greeting card industry," the GCA predicts.

FOR MORE INFORMATION

For information on the industry and artist and writer guidelines, check out the following Web site

Greeting Card Association
1156 15th Street, NW, Suite 900
Washington, DC 20005-1717
Tel: 202-393-1778
Email: info@greetingcard.org
http://www.greetingcard.org

For information on Hallmark's internship program, visit
Hallmark Cards Inc.
http://www.hallmark.com

Visit your library or bookstore for a copy of the latest edition of Writer's Market *and* Artist & Graphic Designers Market, *or contact*
Writer's Digest Books
http://www.writersdigest.com

INTERVIEW

Sandra Miller-Louden from Pittsburgh, Pennsylvania, has been a greeting card writer since 1986. Her Web site, http://www.greetingcardwriting.com, is the only one exclusively devoted to the subject of greeting card writing. Sandra has written two books and has helped many people fulfill their writing dreams.

Q. What are the main responsibilities of your job?
A. I write the words that go into greeting cards. Since I'm a free-lance greeting card writer (as opposed to a staff or "in-house" writer), I work for many different companies. Many times, companies will send artwork to me and I must provide the verse to go with it. At other times, I create the entire concept—both visual and verse; however (to dispel one of the major myths about greeting card writing), I don't have to draw the visual—I describe it.

Q. What is your typical work day like? Do you interact with many people, whether in person or over the phone/e-mail?
A. My job is completely flexible and no two days—or nights—are the same. (You'll often find me working at 3:00 A.M. if that's when my ideas are flowing). I start by reviewing any approaching deadlines; greeting cards are basically divided into two categories: everyday and seasonal. Depending upon my assignment, I may be writing verses for Thanksgiving in May or Valentine's Day in October. As far as interacting with other people, I often say that 99 percent of all people I "know" in the industry I've

never met. I call them my "phone, fax, and e-mail people." These include editors, writers, artists, and cartoonists across the country and around the world. Writing, especially freelance writing, is often a solitary life

Q. What were your expectations entering this field? Are they much different from the realities?

A. I started out in 1986 writing verses on my dining room table, using my Smith-Corona typewriter—the same typewriter I used in college in 1972. I hoped to make some extra money writing greeting cards; I had always wanted to be a writer, yet with two small children, it was impossible to concentrate on longer works. As I continued to write cards, I tried to find more information on the subject, but there was very little. It was a genre that was almost completely ignored and the information that was out there did not reflect my experiences. I began putting together a course that I later taught at a local community college. As the years passed, others became very interested in my work and I was asked to do interviews, first locally, then nationally. I never expected the positive attention I received. Also, I never expected that there were so many people who would contact me to help make their creative dreams become a reality.

Q. What kind of training did you receive for this position? What did you study in college? Did your education prepare you for this position?

A. I received no specific training for this position. In college, I had a dual major—Spanish and English. However, from the beginning, I've always loved the written word and am totally fascinated with languages and how people use words to communicate. One of my most vivid memories is sitting down at my mother's manual Underwood typewriter and teaching myself how to type by copying sentences from a book I was reading—I absolutely loved the feel of keys under my fingers, as they made words on a sheet of paper. I was fortunate to have very supportive English and Spanish professors both in high school and college who encouraged me to write. I remember in 10th grade, my English teacher wrote on a short story I'd turned in: "Very good, as usual." I think the writing seeds were always there; this single comment started them blooming.

Q. Did you achieve success with your first greeting card submissions?

A. No. In fact, the first time I submitted a batch of greeting card verses to an editor, I didn't even know enough to mark my envelope. The very first batch I sent came back to me with a hand-written note from the editor that said: "Very close. Please feel free to try again." Those eight encouraging words were enough to have me dig in my heels and keep trying. Within three months, I'd sold my first greeting card verse. After that, I learned on my own from my own mistakes and also from asking questions. I'd call editors and ask them what they were looking for and what separated good copy from inadequate writing.

Q. What is the best way to find a job in this field?
A. It's really pretty simple. First, read as many greeting cards as you possibly can. Just stand there and read card after card, not only the traditional rhymed metered verse, but what I've termed "contemporary prose"—the soft, conversational, non-rhyming verse—and of course humor, which is something most editors want today. Don't just think Hallmark or American Greetings; it's tough to break into these companies. There are solid midsize and smaller companies that encourage freelance writers and artists. Do an Internet search for greeting card companies; many of them have their writer's guidelines posted right on their sites. Then come up with some solid ideas and begin submitting them to an editor. When I speak at career days in high schools, students are always amazed that there is no minimum age limit for a freelance greeting card writer. As long as you have a Social Security number, you can send in verses. There are certain formats and rules concerning how to submit; these are often covered in the set of guidelines issued from the company.

Q. What would you say are the most important skills and personal qualities for someone in your career?
A. First, you have to love language. You have to be fascinated with the multitude of expressions, phrases, synonyms, and figurative meanings that populate a language. You should also be a visual person; you should have an eye for what stands out in a picture and be able to build a verse around that picture. For example, if I show you a photograph of three Dalmatian puppies, you might focus on their spots and write something like: "I knew you were cute the minute I spotted you." Second, you have to "write tight." There is no place in greeting card writing for long, drawn-out metaphors or obscure references. Finally, you must

have empathy for human relationships and understand how and why people need to communicate their emotions. Greeting cards are sent at life's most important milestones, whether a birth, anniversary, wedding, graduation, promotion, new home, retirement, death, as well as the many holidays people celebrate: Mother's and Father's Day, Valentine's, Easter, Passover, Christmas, Hanukkah, Kwanzaa, Thanksgiving, etc. As a greeting card writer, you must tap into these occasions and get a real feeling for them. You may not have a daughter, for example, but you must be able to think "daughter thoughts" to write a successful card that would be sent to someone's daughter.

Interpreters and Translators

OVERVIEW

An *interpreter* translates spoken passages of a foreign language into another specified language. The job is often designated by the language interpreted, such as Spanish or Japanese. In addition, many interpreters specialize according to subject matter. For example, *medical interpreters* have extensive knowledge of and experience in the health care field, while *court* or *judiciary interpreters* speak both a second language and the "language" of law. *Interpreters for the deaf*, also known as *sign language interpreters*, aid in the communication between people who are unable to hear and those who can.

In contrast to interpreters, *translators* focus on written materials, such as books, plays, technical or scientific papers, legal documents, laws, treaties, and decrees. A *sight translator* performs a combination of interpreting and translating by reading printed material in one language while reciting it aloud in another.

There are approximately 31,000 interpreters and translators employed in the United States.

HISTORY

Until recently, most people who spoke two languages well enough to interpret and translate did so only on the side, working full time in some other occupation. For example, many diplomats and high-level government officials employed people who were able to serve as interpreters and translators, but only as needed. These employees spent the rest of their time assisting in other ways.

U.S. Rep. Howard Berman, D-CA., left, together with a translator, attends a meeting in El Salvador with the president, right, of the Corporation of Municipalities of El Salvador. *(Associated Press)*

Interpreting and translating as full-time professions have emerged only recently, partly in response to the need for high-speed communication across the globe. The increasing use of complex diplomacy has also increased demand for full-time translating and interpreting professionals. For many years, diplomacy was practiced largely between just two nations. Rarely did conferences involve more than two languages at one time. The League of Nations, established by the Treaty of Versailles in 1919, established a new pattern of communication. Although the language of diplomacy was then considered to be French, diplomatic discussions were carried out in many different languages for the first time.

Since the early 1920s, multinational conferences have become commonplace. Trade and educational conferences are now held with participants of many nations in attendance. Responsible for international diplomacy after the League of Nations dissolved, the United Nations (UN) now employs many full-time interpreters and translators, providing career opportunities for qualified people. In addition, the European Union employs a large number of interpreters.

THE JOB

Although interpreters are needed for a variety of languages and different venues and circumstances, there are only two basic systems of interpretation: simultaneous and consecutive. Spurred in part by the invention and development of electronic sound equipment, simultaneous interpretation has been in use since the charter of the UN.

Simultaneous interpreters are able to convert a spoken sentence instantaneously. Some are so skilled that they are able to complete a sentence in the second language at almost the precise moment that the speaker is conversing in the original language. Such interpreters are usually familiar with the speaking habits of the speaker and can anticipate the way in which the sentence will be completed. The interpreter may also make judgments about the intent of the sentence or phrase from the speaker's gestures, facial expressions, and inflections. While working at a fast pace, the interpreter must be careful not to summarize, edit, or in any way change the meaning of what is being said.

In contrast, *consecutive interpreters* wait until the speaker has paused to convert speech into a second language. In this case, the speaker waits until the interpreter has finished before resuming the speech. Since every sentence is repeated in consecutive interpretation, this method takes longer than simultaneous interpretation.

In both systems, interpreters are placed so that they can clearly see and hear all that is taking place. In formal situations, such as those at the UN and other international conferences, interpreters are often assigned to a glass-enclosed booth. Speeches are transmitted to the booth, and interpreters, in turn, translate the speaker's words into a microphone. Each UN delegate can tune in the voice of the appropriate interpreter. Because of the difficulty of the job, these simultaneous interpreters usually work in pairs, each working 30-minute shifts.

All international conference interpreters are simultaneous interpreters. Many interpreters, however, work in situations other than formal diplomatic meetings. For example, interpreters are needed for negotiations of all kinds, as well as for legal, financial, medical, and business purposes. *Court or judiciary interpreters*, for example, work in courtrooms and at attorney-client meetings, depositions, and witness preparation sessions.

Other interpreters known as *guide or escort interpreters* serve on call, traveling with visitors from foreign countries who are touring the United States. Usually, these language specialists use consecutive interpretation. Their job is to make sure that whatever the visitors say is understood and that they also understand what is being said to them. Still other interpreters accompany groups of U.S. citizens on official tours abroad. On such assignments, they may be sent to any foreign country and might be away from the United States for long periods of time.

Interpreters also work on short-term assignments. Services may be required for only brief intervals, such as for a special conference or single interview with press representatives.

While interpreters focus on the spoken word, translators work with written language. They read and translate novels, plays, essays, nonfiction and technical works, legal documents, records and reports, speeches, and other written material. Translators generally follow a certain set of procedures in their work. They begin by reading the text, taking careful notes on what they do not understand. To translate questionable passages, they look up words and terms in specialized dictionaries and glossaries. They may also do additional reading on the subject to arrive at a better understanding. Finally, they write translated drafts in the target language.

Localization translation is a relatively new specialty. *Localization translators* adapt computer software, Web sites, and other business products for use in a different language or culture.

REQUIREMENTS

High School

If you are interested in becoming an interpreter or translator, you should take a variety of English courses, because most trans-lating work is from a foreign language into English. The study of one or more foreign languages is vital. If you are interested in becoming proficient in one or more of the Romance languages, such as Italian, French, or Spanish, basic courses in Latin will be valuable.

While you should devote as much time as possible to the study of at least one foreign language, other helpful courses include speech, business, cultural studies, humanities, world history, geography, and political science. In fact, any course that empha-sizes the written and/or spoken word will be valuable to aspiring interpreters or translators. In addition, knowledge of a particular subject matter in which you may have interest, such as health, law, or science, will give you a professional edge if you want to specialize. Finally, courses in typing and word processing are recommended, especially if you want to pursue a career as a translator.

Postsecondary Training

Because interpreters and translators need to be proficient in grammar, have an excellent vocabulary in the chosen language, and have sound knowledge in a wide variety of subjects, employers generally require that applicants have at least a bachelor's degree. Scientific and professional interpreters are best qualified if they have graduate degrees.

In addition to language and field-specialty skills, you should take college courses that will allow you to develop effective techniques in public speaking, particularly if you're planning to pursue a career as an interpreter. Courses such as speech and debate will improve your diction and confidence as a public speaker.

Hundreds of colleges and universities in the United States offer degrees in languages. In addition, educational institutions now provide programs and degrees specialized for interpreting and translating. Georgetown University (http://linguistics.georgetown.edu/) offers both undergraduate and graduate programs in linguistics. Graduate degrees in interpretation and translation may be earned at the University of California at Santa Barbara (http://www.ucsb.edu), the University of Puerto Rico (http://www.upr.clu.edu), and the Monterey Institute of International Studies (http://www.miis.edu/languages.html). Many of these programs include both general and specialized courses, such as medical interpretation and legal translation.

Academic programs for the training of interpreters can be found in Europe as well. The University of Geneva's School of Translation and Interpretation (http://www.unige.ch/eti) is highly regarded among professionals in the field.

Certification or Licensing

Although interpreters and translators need not be certified to obtain jobs, employers often show preference to certified applicants. Certification in Spanish, Haitian Creole, and Navajo is also required for interpreters who are employed by federal courts. State and local courts often have their own specific certification requirements. The National Center for State Courts has more information on certification for these workers. Interpreters for the deaf who pass an examination may qualify for either comprehensive or legal certification by the Registry of Interpreters for the Deaf. The U.S. Department of State has a three-test requirement for interpreters. These include simple consecutive interpreting (escort), simultaneous interpreting (court/seminar), and conference-level interpreting (international conferences). Applicants must have several years of foreign language practice, advanced education in the language (preferably abroad), and be fluent in vocabulary for a very broad range of subjects.

Foreign language translators may be granted certification by the American Translators Association (ATA) upon successful completion of required exams. ATA certification is available for translators who translate the following languages into English: Arabic, Croatian, Danish, Dutch, French, German, Hungarian, Italian, Japanese, Polish, Portuguese, Russian, and Spanish. Certification is also available for translators who translate English into the following languages: Chinese, Croatian, Dutch, Finnish, French, German, Hungarian, Italian, Japanese, Polish, Portuguese, Russian, Spanish, and Ukrainian.

Other Requirements

Interpreters should be able to speak at least two languages fluently, without strong accents. They should be knowledgeable of not only the foreign language but also of the culture and social norms of the region or country in which it is spoken. Both interpreters and translators should read daily newspapers in the languages in which they work to keep current in both developments and usage.

Interpreters must have good hearing, a sharp mind, and a strong, clear, and pleasant voice. They must be able to be precise and quick in their translation. In addition to being flexible and versatile in their work, both interpreters and translators should have self-discipline and patience. Above all, they should have an interest in and love of language.

Finally, interpreters must be honest and trustworthy, observing any existing codes of confidentiality at all times. The ethical code of interpreters and translators is a rigid one. They must hold private proceedings in strict confidence. Ethics also demands that interpreters and translators not distort the meaning of the sentences that are spoken or written. No matter how much they may agree or disagree with the speaker or writer, interpreters and translators must be objective in their work. In addition, information they obtain in the process of interpretation or translation must never be passed along to unauthorized people or groups.

EXPLORING

If you have an opportunity to visit the United Nations, you can watch the proceedings to get some idea of the techniques and responsibilities of the job of the interpreter. Occasionally, an international conference session is televised, and the work of the interpreters can be

Profile: Maximilian Berlitz

Maximilian D. Berlitz emigrated from Germany to the United States in 1872. After enjoying a successful career as a private language instructor (in Greek, Latin, and six other European languages), Berlitz became a professor of French and German at the Warner Polytechnic College in Providence, Rhode Island, where at one time he served as the institution's owner, dean, principal, and only professor.

Overworked and in need of an assistant to teach French, Berlitz hired Nicholas Joly—only to later discover that Joly did not speak English. Trying to find a way to both communicate with the Frenchman and use him at the college, Berlitz indicated that Joly should point to objects and act out verbs, while at the same time, naming them in French.

The result? Students began participating in dynamic question-and-answer sessions with Joly—all in elegant French! The formality of the classroom had disappeared. In its place, Berlitz found that he had quite accidentally developed an innovative teaching technique that kept students alert and interested. Today, people can go to over 300 Berlitz centers around the world in order to learn languages needed for business or personal travel.

observed. You should note, however, that interpreters who work at these conferences are in the top positions of the vocation. Not everyone may aspire to such jobs. The work of interpreters and translators is usually less public, but not necessarily less interesting.

If you have adequate skills in a foreign language, you might consider traveling in a country in which the language is spoken. If you can converse easily and without a strong accent and can interpret to others who may not understand the language well, you may have what it takes to work as an interpreter or translator.

For any international field, it is important that you familiarize yourself with other cultures. You can even arrange to regularly correspond with a pen pal in a foreign country. You may also want to join a school club that focuses on a particular language, such as the French Club or the Spanish Club. If no such clubs exist, consider forming one. Student clubs can allow you to hone your foreign language speaking and writing skills and learn about other cultures.

Finally, participating on a speech or debate team can allow you to practice your public speaking skills, increase your confidence, and polish your overall appearance by working on eye contact, gestures, facial expressions, tone, and other elements used in public speaking.

EMPLOYERS

There are approximately 31,000 interpreters and translators in the United States. Although many interpreters and translators work for government or international agencies, some are employed by private firms. Large import-export companies often have interpreters or translators on their payrolls, although these employees generally perform additional duties for the firm. International banks, companies, organizations, and associations often employ both interpreters and translators to facilitate communication. In addition, translators and interpreters work at publishing houses, schools, bilingual newspapers, radio and television stations, airlines, shipping companies, law firms, and scientific and medical operations.

While translators are employed nationwide, a large number of interpreters find work in New York and Washington, D.C. Among the largest employers of interpreters and translators are the United Nations, the World Bank, the U.S. Department of State, the Bureau of the Census, the CIA, the FBI, the Library of Congress, the Red Cross, the YMCA, and the armed forces.

Finally, many interpreters and translators work independently in private practice. These self-employed professionals must be disciplined and driven, since they must handle all aspects of the business such as scheduling work and billing clients.

STARTING OUT

Most interpreters and translators begin as part-time freelancers until they gain experience and contacts in the field. Individuals can apply for jobs directly to the hiring firm, agency, or organization. Many of these employers advertise available positions in the classified section of the newspaper or on the Internet. In addition, contact your college career services office and language department to inquire about job leads.

While many opportunities exist, top interpreting and translating jobs are hard to obtain since the competition for these higher-profile positions is fierce. You may be wise to develop supplemental skills that can be attractive to employers while refining your interpreting and translating techniques. The UN, for example, employs administrative assistants who can take shorthand and transcribe notes in two or more languages. The UN also hires tour guides who speak more than one language. Such positions can be initial steps toward your future career goals.

ADVANCEMENT

Competency in language determines the speed of advancement for interpreters and translators. Job opportunities and promotions are plentiful for those who have acquired great proficiency in languages. However, interpreters and translators need to constantly work and study to keep abreast of the changing linguistic trends for a given language. The constant addition of new vocabulary for technological advances, inventions, and processes keep languages fluid. Those who do not keep up with changes will find that their communication skills become quickly outdated.

Interpreters and translators who work for government agencies advance by clearly defined grade promotions. Those who work for other organizations can aspire to become chief interpreters or chief translators, or reviewers who check the work of others.

Although advancement in the field is generally slow, interpreters and translators will find many opportunities to succeed as freelancers. Some can even establish their own bureaus or agencies.

EARNINGS

Earnings for interpreters and translators vary depending on experience, skills, number of languages used, and employers. According to the U.S. Department of Labor, in 2005 salaried interpreters and translators earned a median salary of $34,800. The lowest-paid 10 percent of interpreters and translators earn less than $20,540. The highest-paid 10 percent earn over $61,770.

In government, trainee interpreters and translators generally begin at the GS-5 rating, earning from $25,195 to $32,755 a year in 2006. Those with a college degree can start at the higher GS-7 level, earning from $31,209 to $40,569. With an advanced degree, trainees begin at the GS-9 ($38,175 to $49,632), GS-10 ($42,040 to $54,649), or GS-11 level ($46,189 to $60,049).

Interpreters who are employed by the United Nations work under a salary structure called the Common System. In 2006, UN short-term interpreters (workers employed for a duration of 60 days or less) had daily gross pay of $309 (Grade I) or $474.50 (Grade II). UN short-term translators and revisers had daily gross pay of $183.50 (Translator I), $225.70 (Translator II), $267.65 (Translator III/Reviser I), $301.20 (Translator IV/Reviser II), or $334.80 (Reviser III).

Interpreters and translators who work on a freelance basis usually charge by the word, the page, the hour, or the project. Freelance interpreters for international conferences or meetings can

Advice from the Trenches

If you are considering a career as a translator or interpreter but wondering whether you've got what it takes, here is some advice from those currently in the field:

- Make sure that you love the language, both spoken and written.
- Develop your people skills.
- Keep abreast of new developments affecting your field or business.
- Ask your peers to periodically review your work.
- Learn how to negotiate rates, work within deadlines, and handle revisers.
- Stay in step with advances in online resources, as well as search technologies.
- Invest in dictionaries, grammar books, and other resource materials.
- Have self-discipline and patience.
- Don't bite off more than you can chew.
- Aim for the most accurate translation or interpretation possible.
- Learn how to type!
- Maintain high professional standards.
- Exhibit cultural sensitivity and awareness.

earn between $300 and $500 a day from the U.S. government. By the hour, freelance translators usually earn between $15 and $35; however, rates vary depending on the language and the subject matter. Book translators work under contract with publishers. These contracts cover the fees that are to be paid for translating work as well as royalties, advances, penalties for late payments, and other provisions.

Interpreters and translators working in a specialized field have high earning potential. According to the National Association of Judiciary Interpreters and Translators, the federal courts pay $305 per day for court interpreters. Most work as freelancers, earning annual salaries from $30,000 to $100,000 a year.

Interpreters who work for the deaf also may work on a freelance basis, earning anywhere from $12 to $40 an hour, according to the Registry of Interpreters for the Deaf. Those employed with an agency, government organization, or school system can earn up to $30,000 to start; in urban areas, $40,000 to $50,000 a year.

Depending on the employer, interpreters and translators often enjoy such benefits as health and life insurance, pension plans, and paid vacation and sick days.

WORK ENVIRONMENT

Interpreters and translators work under a wide variety of circumstances and conditions. As a result, most do not have typical nine-to-five schedules.

Conference interpreters probably have the most comfortable physical facilities in which to work. Their glass-enclosed booths are well lit and temperature controlled. Court or judiciary interpreters work in courtrooms or conference rooms, while interpreters for the deaf work at educational institutions as well as a wide variety of other locations.

Interpreters who work for escort or tour services are often required to travel for long periods of time. Their schedules are dictated by the group or person for whom they are interpreting. A freelance interpreter may work out of one city or be assigned anywhere in the world as needed.

Translators usually work in offices, although many spend considerable time in libraries and research centers. Freelance translators often work at home, using their own personal computers, the Internet, dictionaries, and other resource materials.

While both interpreting and translating require flexibility and versatility, interpreters in particular, especially those who work for international congresses or courts, may experience considerable stress and fatigue. Knowing that a great deal depends upon their absolute accuracy in interpretation can be a weighty responsibility.

OUTLOOK

Employment opportunities for interpreters and translators are expected to grow faster than the average through 2014, according to the U.S. Department of Labor. However, competition for available positions will be fierce. With the explosion of such technologies as the Internet, lightning-fast Internet connections, and videoconferencing, global communication has taken great strides. In short, the world has become smaller, so to speak, creating a demand for professionals to aid in the communication between people of different languages and cultural backgrounds.

In addition to new technological advances, demographic factors will fuel demand for translators and interpreters. Although some immigrants who come to the United States assimilate easily with respect to culture and language, many have difficulty learning English. As immigration to the United States continues to increase, interpreters and translators will be needed to help immigrants function in an English-speaking society. According to Ann Macfarlane, past president of the American Translators Association, "community interpreting" for immigrants and refugees is a challenging area requiring qualified language professionals.

Another demographic factor influencing the interpreting and translating fields is the growth in overseas travel. Americans on average are spending an increasing amount of money on travel, especially to foreign countries. The resulting growth of the travel industry will create a need for interpreters to lead tours, both at home and abroad.

In addition to leisure travel, business travel is spurring the need for more translators and interpreters. With workers traveling abroad in growing numbers to attend meetings, conferences, and seminars with overseas clients, interpreters and translators will be needed to help bridge both the language and cultural gaps.

While no more than a few thousand interpreters and translators are employed in the largest markets (the federal government and international organizations), other job options exist. The medical field, for example, will provide many jobs for language professionals, translating such products as pharmaceutical inserts, research papers, and medical reports for insurance companies. Interpreters will also be needed to provide non-English speakers with language assistance in health care settings. Opportunities exist for qualified individuals in law, trade and business, health care, tourism, recreation, and the government. The American with Disabilities Act and other laws mandates that interpreters for the deaf and hard of hearing are required in some situations. This means that opportunities for interpreters for the deaf should be favorable.

The U.S. Department of Labor predicts that employment growth will be limited for conference interpreters and literary translators.

FOR MORE INFORMATION

For information on careers in literary translation, contact
American Literary Translators Association
University of Texas-Dallas
Box 830688, Mail Station JO51
Richardson, TX 75083-0688
http://www.literarytranslators.org

For more on the translating and interpreting professions, including information on accreditation, contact
American Translators Association
225 Reinekers Lane, Suite 590
Alexandria, VA 22314-2875
Tel: 703-683-6100
Email: ata@atanet.org
http://www.atanet.org

For more information on court interpreting and certification, contact
National Association of Judiciary Interpreters and Translators
603 Stewart Street, Suite 610
Seattle, WA 98101-1229
Tel: 206-367-2300
Email: headquarters@najit.org
http://www.najit.org

For information on interpreter training programs for working with the deaf and certification, contact
Registry of Interpreters for the Deaf
333 Commerce Street
Alexandria, VA 22314-2801
Tel: 703-838-0030
Email: membership@rid.org
http://www.rid.org

For information on union membership for freelance interpreters and translators, contact
Translators and Interpreters Guild
962 Wayne Avenue, #500
Silver Spring, MD 20910-4432
Tel: 301-563-6450
Email: info@ttig.org
http://www.ttig.org

Medical Transcriptionists

QUICK FACTS

School Subjects
Biology
English
Health

Personal Skills
Communication/ideas
Technical/scientific

Work Environment
Primarily indoors
Primarily one location

Minimum Education Level
Some postsecondary training

Salary Range
$20,710 to $29,080 to
$41,100+

Certification or Licensing
Recommended

Outlook
Faster than the average

DOT
N/A

GOE
09.07.02

NOC
1244

O*NET-SOC
31-9094.00

OVERVIEW

Doctors and other health care professionals often make tape recordings documenting what happened during their patients' appointments or surgical procedures. *Medical transcriptionists* listen to these tapes and transcribe, or type, reports of what the doctor said. The reports are then included in patients' charts. Medical transcriptionists work in a variety of health care settings, including hospitals, clinics, and doctors' offices, as well as for transcription companies or out of their own homes. There are approximately 105,000 medical transcriptionists working in the United States. Medical transcriptionists are also called *medical transcribers*, *medical stenographers*, or *medical language specialists*.

HISTORY

Health care documentation dates back to the beginnings of medical treatment. Doctors used to keep their own handwritten records of a patient's medical history and treatment. After 1900, medical stenographers took on this role. Stenographers worked alongside doctors, writing down doctors' reports in shorthand. This changed with the invention of the dictating machine, which led to the development of the career of medical transcription.

The first commercial dictating machine, using a wax cylinder record, was produced in 1887. It was based on Thomas A. Edison's phonograph invented in 1877. Technology has come a long way since then. Recent advances in the field include Internet transcription capabilities and voice (or speech) recognition software. The latter electronically transcribes recorded spoken word, which means that a medical transcriptionist does not have to type out all the dictation. Given the complexity of medical terminology, however, voice recognition programs are likely to make mistakes, so there is still plenty of work for the medical transcriptionist, who must carefully proofread the report to catch and correct any errors.

THE JOB

Medical transcriptionists transcribe (type into printed format) a dictated (oral) report recorded by a doctor or another health care professional. They work for primary care physicians as well as health care professionals in various medical specialties, including cardiology, immunology, oncology, podiatry, radiology, and urology. The medical transcriptionist usually types up the report while listening to the recording through a transcriber machine's headset, using a foot pedal to stop or rewind the recording as necessary. Some doctors dictate over the telephone, and others use the Internet.

The report consists of information gathered during a patient's office appointment or hospital visit and covers the patient's medical history and treatment. Doctors dictate information about patient consultations, physical examinations, results from laboratory work or X rays, medical tests, psychiatric evaluations, patient diagnosis and prognosis, surgical procedures, a patient's hospital stay and discharge, autopsies, and so on. Often doctors will use abbreviations while dictating. The medical transcriptionist must type out the full names of those abbreviations.

Because the report becomes a permanent part of a patient's medical record and is referred to by the same doctor or other members of the patient's health care team during future office visits or when determining future medical treatment, it must be accurate. This includes dates and the spelling of medications, procedures, diseases, medical instruments and supplies, and laboratory values.

After typing up a report, medical transcriptionists review it and make corrections to grammar, punctuation, and spelling. They read it to be sure it is clear, consistent, and complete and does not contain any errors. Medical transcriptionists are expected to edit for clarity and make grammatical corrections; therefore, the final report does not need to be identical to the original dictation in those respects.

Being a medical transcriptionist is not all about typing and proofreading. Medical transcriptionists must be very familiar with medical terminology. When recording their reports, doctors use medical terms that are relevant to a patient's condition and treatment. Such terms might be names of diseases or medications. Medical transcriptionists understand what these medical terms mean and how they are spelled. They understand enough about various diseases and their symptoms, treatments, and prognoses as to be able to figure out what a doctor is saying if the recording is unclear. They have a good understanding of medicine and are familiar with human anatomy and physiology. If what the doctor says on the tape is not clear, a medical transcriptionist often has to determine the appropriate word or words based on the context. However, medical transcriptionists never guess when it comes to medications, conditions, medical history, and treatments. A patient could receive improper and even damaging treatment if a diagnosis is made based on a report containing errors. Medical transcriptionists contact the doctor if they are uncertain or they leave a blank in the report, depending on the employer's or client's expectations and guidelines. After the medical transcriptionist reviews the report, it is given to the doctor, who also reviews it and then signs it if it is acceptable—or returns it to the transcriptionist for correction, if necessary. Once it has been signed, the report is placed in the patient's permanent medical file.

Many medical transcriptionists use voice recognition software to electronically create documents from oral dictation, eliminating much of their typing work. Medical transcriptionists still have to review the transcription carefully for accuracy and format.

While some transcriptionists only do transcribing, other transcriptionists, often those who work in doctors' offices or clinics, may have additional responsibilities. They may deal with patients, answer the phone, handle the mail, and perform other clerical tasks. And transcriptionists may be asked to file or deliver the reports to other doctors, lawyers, or other people who request them.

A growing number of medical transcriptionists work out of their homes, either telecommuting as employees or subcontractors, or as self-employed workers. As technology becomes more sophisticated, this trend is likely to continue. Medical transcriptionists who work out of their homes have some degree of mobility and can live where they choose, taking their jobs with them. These workers must keep up-to-date with their medical resources and equipment. Because terminology continues to change, medical transcriptionists regularly buy new editions of the standard medical resources.

REQUIREMENTS

High School

English and grammar classes are important in preparing you to become a medical transcriptionist. Focus on becoming a better speller. If you understand the meanings of word prefixes and suffixes (many of which come from Greek and Latin), it will be easier for you to learn medical terminology, since many terms are formed by adding a prefix and/or a suffix to a word or root. If your high school offers Greek or Latin classes, take one; otherwise, try to take Greek or Latin when you continue your studies after high school.

Biology and health classes will give you a solid introduction to the human body and how it functions, preparing you to take more advanced classes in anatomy and physiology after you graduate. Be sure to learn how to type by taking a class or teaching yourself. Practice typing regularly to build up your speed and accuracy. Word processing and computer classes are also useful.

Postsecondary Training

Some junior, community, and business colleges and vocational schools have medical transcription programs. You can also learn the business of medical transcription by taking a correspondence course. To be accepted into a medical transcription program, you might need to have a minimum typing speed. The American Association for Medical Transcription (AAMT) recommends that medical transcriptionists complete a two-year program offering an associate's degree, but this is not necessary for you to find a job.

You should take courses in English grammar as well as medical terminology, anatomy, physiology, and pharmacology. Some of the more specific classes you might take include Medicolegal Concepts and Ethics, Human Disease and Pathophysiology, Health Care Records Management, and Medical Grammar and Editing. Certain programs offer on-the-job training, which will help when you are looking for full-time employment.

The AAMT has a mentoring program for students who are studying medical transcription. Students can make important contacts in the field and learn much from experienced professionals.

Certification or Licensing

The Medical Transcription Certification Commission (MTCC) of the AAMT administers a certification examination that tests applicants on their medical transcription-related knowledge and transcription performance. Those who pass the exam become certified medical transcriptionists (CMTs). Certification is good for three years, at which point recertification is necessary to keep the CMT designation. At least 30 hours of continuing education credits are required every three years. (There are also other requirements, which are detailed at the AAMT Web site, http://www.aamt.org.)

While medical transcriptionists do not need to be certified to find a job, it is highly recommended as a sign of achievement and professionalism. CMTs are more likely to find employment and earn higher salaries.

Other Requirements

A love of language and grammar is an important quality, and accuracy and attention to detail are absolute musts for a medical transcriptionist. It is essential that you correctly type information as spoken by the doctor on his or her tape recording. You must be able to sift through background sounds on the tape and accurately record what the doctor says. Doctors dictate at the same time they are with a patient or later from their office or maybe even as they go about their daily routine, perhaps while eating, driving in traffic, or walking along a busy street. In each of these cases, the recording will likely include background noises or conversations that at times drown out or make unclear what the doctor is saying.

Many doctors grew up outside of the United States and do not speak English as their first language, so they may not have a thorough understanding of English or they may speak with an accent. You must have a good ear to be able to decipher what these doctors are saying.

In addition to having accurate typing skills, you will also need to type quickly if you want to earn higher wages and get more clients. A solid understanding of word processing software will help you to be more productive. An example of this is the use of macros, or keystroke combinations that are used to substitute for repetitive actions, such as typing the same long, hard-to-spell word or phrase time and again. If you suffer from repetitive strain injuries, then this would not be a suitable profession.

Flexibility is also important because you must be able to adapt to the different skills and needs of various health care professionals.

Medical transcriptionists should be able to concentrate and be prepared to sit in one place for long periods at a time, either typing or reading. For this reason, it is important that you take regular breaks. An ability to work independently will help you whether you are self-employed or have an office position, since you do most of your work sitting at a computer.

Medical transcriptionists are required to keep patient records confidential, just as doctors are, so integrity and discretion are important.

EXPLORING

There is plenty of accessible reading material aimed at medical transcriptionists. This is a good way to learn more about the field and decide if it sounds interesting to you. Several of the Web sites listed at the end of this article feature self-tests and articles about medical transcription. Marylou Bunting, a home-based certified medical transcriptionist, recommends that you get a medical dictionary and PDR (*Physicians' Desk Reference*) to familiarize yourself with terminology. See if your local library has the *Journal of the American Association for Medical Transcription* and browse through some issues. The Internet is a great resource for would-be medical transcriptionists. Find a bulletin board or mailing list and talk to professionals in the field, perhaps conducting an informational interview.

Bunting also suggests that you "put yourself in a medical setting as soon and as often as you can." Ask if your doctor can use your help in any way or apply for a volunteer position at a local hospital. Ask to be assigned to the hospital's medical records department, which won't give you the opportunity to transcribe, but will give you some experience dealing with medical records.

EMPLOYERS

According to the *Occupational Outlook Handbook*, there are about 105,000 medical transcriptionists working in the United States. About 40 percent work in hospitals and 30 percent work in doctors' offices and clinics. Others work for laboratories, home health care services, medical centers, colleges and universities, medical libraries, insurance companies, transcription companies, temp agencies, and even veterinary facilities. Medical transcriptionists can also find government jobs, with public health or veterans hospitals.

STARTING OUT

It can be difficult to get started in this field, especially if you do not have any work experience. Some medical transcriptionists start out working as administrative assistants or receptionists in doctors' offices. They become acquainted with medical terminology and office procedures, and they make important contacts in the medical profession. According to AAMT, a smaller doctor's office may be more apt to hire an inexperienced medical transcriptionist than a hospital or transcription service would be.

Marylou Bunting recommends that you try to get an informal apprenticeship position since on-the-job experience seems to be a prerequisite for most jobs. Or perhaps you can find an internship position with a transcription company. Once you have some experience, you can look for another position through classified ads, job search agencies, or Internet resources. You can also find job leads through word-of-mouth and professional contacts. The AAMT Web site features job postings. In fact, AAMT is an invaluable resource for the medical transcriptionist. Local chapters hold periodic meetings, which is a good way to network with other professionals in the field.

ADVANCEMENT

There are few actual advancement opportunities for medical transcriptionists. Those who become faster and more accurate will have an easier time securing better-paying positions or lining up new clients. Skilled and experienced medical transcriptionists can become supervisors of transcription departments or managers of transcription companies, or they might even form their own transcription companies. Some also become teachers, consultants, or authors or editors of books on the subject of medical transcription.

EARNINGS

Medical transcriptionists are paid in a variety of ways, depending on the employer or client. Payment might be made based on the number of hours worked or the number of lines transcribed. Monetary incentives might be offered to hourly transcriptionists achieving a high rate of production.

The U.S. Department of Labor reports that in 2005 the lowest-paid 10 percent of all medical transcriptionists earned an annual salary of $20,710, and the highest-paid 10 percent earned $41,100, annually. The median annual salary was $29,080. Medical transcriptionists who worked in hospitals earned $30,270 annually and those who worked in offices and clinics of medical doctors earned $29,380. Medical transcriptionists who are certified earn higher average salaries than transcriptionists who have not earned certification.

Medical transcriptionists working in a hospital or company setting can expect to receive the usual benefits, including paid vacation, sick days, and health insurance. Tuition reimbursement and 401(k) plans may also be offered. Home-based medical transcriptionists who are employed by a company may be entitled to the same benefits that in-house staff members get. It is important to check with each individual company to be sure. Self-employed medical transcriptionists have to make arrangements for their own health and retirement plans and other benefits.

WORK ENVIRONMENT

Most medical transcriptionists work in an office setting, either at their employer's place of business or in their own homes. They generally sit at desks in front of computers and have transcribers or dictation machines and medical reference books at hand. Home-based workers and sometimes even office workers must invest a substantial amount of money in reference books and equipment on an ongoing basis, to keep up with changes in medical terminology and technology.

Transcriptionists who are not self-employed usually put in a 40-hour week. Some medical transcriptionists working in hospitals are assigned to the second or third shift. Independent contractors, on the other hand, clock their hours when they have work to do. Sometimes this will be part time or on the weekends or at night. If they are busy enough, some work more hours than in the normal workweek.

Because medical transcriptionists spend such a long time typing at a computer, the risk of repetitive stress injuries is present. Other physical problems may also occur, including eyestrain from staring at a computer screen and back or neck pain from sitting in one position for long periods at a time.

OUTLOOK

As Internet security issues are resolved, its use for receiving dictation and returning transcriptions will likely become more popular.

A Medical Transcriptionist's Bookshelf

Medical transcriptionists have to keep up to date with the practice of medicine. A well-rounded library includes the latest editions of a medical dictionary, a drug reference, a medical abbreviations book, a style and grammar handbook, and books on anatomy and pathology. Here is a list of some of the titles you might find on a medical transcriptionist's bookshelf:

Avila-Weil, Donna, and Mary Glaccum. *The Independent Medical Transcriptionist: The Comprehensive Guidebook for Career Success in a Medical Transcription Business*. Windsor, Calif.: Rayve Productions, 2002.

Byrne, Linda A. et al. *The AAMT Book of Style for Medical Transcription*. 2d ed. Modesto, Calif.: American Association for Medical Transcription, 2002.

Dorland, W. A. Newman. *Dorland's Illustrated Medical Dictionary*. Philadelphia: W. B. Saunders Co., 2007.

Drake, Ellen, and Sheila B. Sloane. *Sloane's Medical Word Book*. Philadelphia: W. B. Saunders Co., 2001.

Gray, Henry, and Carmine D. Clemente, eds. *Gray's Anatomy of the Human Body*. 30th ed. Philadelphia: Lippincott, Williams & Wilkins, 2007.

Medical Transcription: Fundamentals and Practice. 3d ed. Upper Saddle River, N.J.: Prentice Hall, 2006.

The Merck Manual of Medical Information. 2d ed. New York: Simon & Schuster, 2003.

Physicians' Desk Reference (PDR). Stamford, Conn.: Thomson Healthcare, 2006.

Stedman's Abbreviations, Acronyms and Symbols. Philadelphia: Lippincott, Williams & Wilkins, 2005.

The Internet offers a quick way to communicate and transfer documents, which is useful for medical transcriptionists who work far away from their employers or clients. As voice recognition technology improves and better recognizes complex medical terminology, it, too, will be used more and medical transcriptionists will do less typing.

Even with these technological advances, there will continue to be a need for medical transcriptionists. They will still have to review electronically created documents. And given that people are living longer, they will require more medical tests and procedures, which will all need to be documented and transcribed.

The U.S. Department of Labor reports that employment of medical transcriptionists is expected to grow faster than the average through 2014.

FOR MORE INFORMATION

AAMT, a professional organization for medical transcriptionists, provides many online resources, including suggestions on how to prepare for a career in medical transcription, a career overview, tips for students, and tips for those interested in becoming self-employed medical transcriptionists.
American Association for Medical Transcription
4230 Kiernan Avenue, Suite 130
Modesto, CA 95356-9322
Tel: 800-982-2182
Email: aamt@aamt.org
http://www.aamt.org

This publication contains an assortment of articles of interest to health information management professionals, including medical transcriptionists.
Advance for Health Information Professionals
http://www.advanceforhim.com

This Web site features articles and resources for medical transcriptionists and those wanting to learn more about the field.
Keeping Abreast of Medical Transcription
http://wwma.com/kamt

For an overview of the job, several language resources and tests, and sample reports, visit
Medword—Medical Transcription
http://www.medword.com

This networking resource for professionals includes discussion forums and interviews.
MT Daily
http://www.mtdaily.com

See this Web site for an extensive glossary, a huge list of "stumper terms" for medical transcriptionists, links to other medical-related dictionaries and resources, sample operative reports, book suggestions, chat forums, and classified ads.

MT Desk
http://www.mtdesk.com

This site features preparatory materials, including quizzes, proofreading tests, and crossword puzzles; articles about getting started; tips on transcribing, punctuation, and grammar; and listings of recommended resources.

MT Monthly and Review of Systems
http://www.medicaltranscriptioncenter.net

Online Journalists

OVERVIEW

Online journalists research and write content for Internet Web sites. They may be full-time salaried workers or employed on a freelance basis. They may work for online publications, professional associations, businesses with an online presence, and the government. Some writers are volunteer online columnists or contributors and do not get paid for their writing.

HISTORY

One of the greatest things about the World Wide Web is that people can gain access to information from around the world with a click of a mouse. Whether one wants to know about international news, current events, fitness trends, or recipes, the Internet has a wealth of information on the topic. This would not be possible without the work of writers such as online journalists.

As newspapers, journals, businesses, and organizations continue to make their presence known on the Internet, job opportunities will continue to open up for writers to create, edit, and update the content of sites. The popularity of news sites such as The Wall Street Journal Online (http://online.wsj.com/public/us) and CNN.com (http://www.cnn.com) prove that there is a market for dependable, timely online news outlets.

THE JOB

The work of online journalists is published on Web sites in online publications. They may write articles for e-zines (online magazines), press releases that are posted on company or society Web sites, or stories for online newspapers. The online journalist must pay special attention to the tone and length of an article. Few readers will scroll through screen after screen of text.

"Writing for the Web is somewhat different than print journalism," says Maria Erspamer, an editorial director for a Web site and a freelance online journalist in Venice, California. "The attention span of online readers is not as great." Erspamer explains that the online journalist must be able to write in a style that provides news while also engaging the reader's interest. "You need to use a standard voice, meaning that there must be a mix of entertainment and information in your writing. Along with that you need to be concise, since many online readers scan the content."

While online journalists do not need to be computer geniuses, they do need to know what computer and Internet tools can make their articles more interesting. Frequently, online journalists incorporate highlighted key words, lists, pop-up boxes or windows, and hypertext links in their articles. These items make the articles visually appealing and easy to read. In addition, such things as hypertext links and pop-up windows allow the journalist to include a depth of information in articles that might otherwise be short and superficial.

Stacie Kilgore of Peachtree City, Georgia, is a senior analyst and online journalist for a major research and consulting firm. She believes that, in a sense, writing for the online audience is easier than writing for a print source. "I can include more information," she says. "For instance, in my articles I can include pop-up windows that explain a terminology or concept. This allows me to reach a wider audience. I can write for the more experienced audience and still be able to reach the newcomers or those with limited technical knowledge."

Online journalists work for publishing companies of various sizes. These companies may be businesses that have been built solely around Web journalism, such as the e-zine *Salon*, or they may be traditional publishing companies that have also developed a Web presence, such as *The New York Times* or *Entertainment Weekly*. Online journalists may also work for news organizations, research firms, and other businesses that have Web sites where articles are published. Some online journalists are full-time salaried employees of companies, while others may work on a freelance basis. As a freelancer, the online journalist runs his or her own business. The freelancer may get an assignment from a company to write a particular article, or the freelancer may write an article and then attempt to sell it to a company for publication.

Erspamer enjoys her freelance work because it allows her the opportunity to write about topics that interest her. "I always have ideas for articles," she says, "and the Internet offers a wealth of material and creative venues." When Erspamer writes an article that she hopes to sell to an online publishing company, she must research the topic, find out what other articles on the subject have already been published, decide on the marketability of her article idea, and write about the topic in a new and interesting way that will make her article stand out from others. Freelancers also need business skills to keep track of their financial accounts and market their work. Erspamer notes, "With freelancing it is sometimes difficult to retrieve payment for articles I have written. Sometimes I have to be a forceful business person as well as a journalist."

Both freelance and salaried online journalists must be organized and able to work under time pressures. The deadlines for online journalists can be similar to those for print journalists. Erspamer notes, "Some articles are time-sensitive, meaning that they must be written and disseminated quickly or the information will no longer be valuable." This time-sensitive factor is especially true for those working for news organizations. Deadlines will be tight, particularly since readers turn to Web sites expecting to find the most up-to-date information possible.

"I have to be very deadline conscious in my job," Erspamer says. When she receives assignments from online publishers, she reviews the articles to be written and prioritizes them according to the assigned deadlines. After she has completed this step, she says, "I do Internet research on the subject, seek out experts to interview to provide backup information, and then write the articles in the order of their importance and the deadlines." After the articles are written, they are reviewed and turned in to the publisher.

As an online editor, Erspamer solicits writers whose expertise matches the material she needs written. Her responsibilities include overseeing the project to its completion. "I manage the materials and make sure they are all written in the voice that speaks for our product and company," she says.

Many people working in online writing view the speed at which an article can go from the concept stage to the published stage as an asset. "I like being an online editor because I like being involved with creating a voice for the Web site, overseeing the written content, and seeing immediate feedback," Erspamer says.

Kilgore also takes satisfaction from publishing her writing online. "What I write gets dispersed quickly, yet it is archived," she says. "The article is long-standing, and readers can retrieve it quickly through a search, so essentially my articles live on forever."

One drawback to the online journalist's career is that many Internet companies are not well established, and thus job security is minimal.

However, for those writers interested in being on the cutting edge of technology and having their writing available to millions, the online journalism field is the right place to be.

REQUIREMENTS

High School

If you are considering a career as an online journalist, you should take college preparatory classes while in high school. Concentrate on English classes that allow you to develop your research and writing skills. Take computer classes that teach you to use word processing programs, graphics, and the Internet. If your school offers journalism classes, take these to develop another writing style and learn about publications. To prepare for college and have the broad educational background any writer needs, take mathematics, science, and history classes.

Postsecondary Training

Many online journalists have bachelor's degrees in journalism. You may also be able to enter the field with a degree in English or communications. While there are currently no specific online journalism degrees available, a number of universities have journalism programs offering courses in online journalism. Traditional journalism courses usually cover such topics as basic reporting and copyediting, press law and ethics, and history of journalism.

In addition to your journalism studies, continue to take computer classes. Learning HTML, a Web site authoring language, can also be helpful to an online journalist and may qualify you for other writing and editing opportunities. It is also essential that you learn the most popular software programs and office tools that relate to the writing profession.

Finally, one of the most beneficial things you can do during your college years is to gain hands-on experience through a journalism internship or summer job at a publishing company. Working in online journalism, naturally, is best. But even if you have an internship at a traditional print publication, you will gain valuable experience. Some schools' career services offices or journalism departments have information on such internships.

Other Requirements

If you want to be an online journalist, you will need good research skills. You must have a love for learning and enjoy searching for new information. You must have the desire and initiative to keep up on new technology and the changes that are constantly taking place on the Internet. You must also have good communication skills and the ability to listen and interpret what others are saying. All journalists must have good grammar, spelling, and editing skills. Online journalists, in particular, must know how to write concisely. You must also be organized, self-motivated, and able to meet strict deadlines. Because you will deal with many different people in various lines of work, you must have good interpersonal skills.

EXPLORING

To explore journalism while you are still in high school, join your school's newspaper staff. As a reporter, you will have the experience of researching, interviewing people, and writing articles on deadline. If you do layout work with the computer, you will gain experience using publishing software. Another way to explore your interest in writing is to join a local writing group. Your high school, local library, or community center may sponsor writing groups; in addition, these groups may be advertised in the local newspaper. Contact your local newspaper to arrange for an informational interview with a journalist there. If the newspaper has an online version, ask to speak with someone who works on the online publication. During the interview you will have the opportunity to ask a professional what the best parts of their job are, what type of education and experience he or she has, and other questions that interest you.

To explore the computer and Internet aspects of this career, surf the Web on a regular basis to check out sites and read their content. Join a computer users' group at your school or in the area. If your high school has a Web site, volunteer to update the site periodically with reports on school news and events. You could also work on updating the information posted on the Web sites of other organizations you are involved with, such as a group at school or at your church, temple, or mosque.

If you have a particular interest in a subject or hobby, write some articles and submit them to an appropriate Web site for publication. Many Web sites do not pay for unsolicited material; however, getting an article published is an excellent way to break into the field and also to determine if an online journalism career is something you wish to pursue.

EMPLOYERS

Online journalists may work for publishing companies that only produce online publications, for traditional publishing companies that also have a Web presence, and for news organizations, research firms, or other businesses that have Web sites. Online journalists may also work as freelancers, writing articles for various companies and sites.

Companies involved in online publishing are located across the country; company sizes vary. While large and well-known companies, such as *The New York Times*, attract a large share of the online audience, the ease and affordability of online publishing is allowing many smaller companies to produce online publications.

STARTING OUT

To get started in this field, a budding journalist may want to write articles and attempt to get them published. According to Maria Erspamer, "The online market is more open to new, unpublished writers than traditional markets. Try to get published on these sites. Many online sites pay little or nothing for articles; however, they will usually provide clips of published work, which helps a new writer develop a portfolio and credibility."

Some online journalists believe that those interested in the career will benefit from starting out in print journalism and then transferring their skills to online journalism. Those starting out in either print journalism or online journalism usually begin in the position of editorial assistant. Although the editorial assistant job is relatively low paying, it will give you the opportunity to learn the business and usually provides you with your first writing assignments. Talented and hard-working assistants will typically work their way up to full-fledged reporters.

Your college career services office and journalism or communications department should be able to give you help with your job search. In addition, contacts that you make during an internship or summer job may provide employment leads. You can also apply for employment directly to publishing companies or other companies with Web publications. Use classified ads and the Internet as resources when looking for job openings.

ADVANCEMENT

Some journalists believe it is easier to move through the ranks as an online journalist than as a traditional journalist working for a newspaper, TV station, or radio station. One reason for this is that online journalism is a relatively new and growing field offering many opportunities. Advancement will also depend on an individual's goals. A salaried journalist may consider it an advancement to do freelance work full time. A full-time freelancer may advance by publishing more articles and expanding his or her client base. Other advancements may mean a shift in career focus away from journalism. Maria Erspamer explains, "There can be career transition or advancement from a writer to a content developer for a Web company." Another online advancement can be moving up to the position of editor or communications director. "You may also advance to working in multimedia and using your creative and writing skills as a creative director," Erspamer adds.

Some online journalists advance their careers by transferring to the print medium and working their way up the ranks of a newspaper or magazine.

EARNINGS

There are no official salary figures currently available for online journalists. However, as with other Web-related jobs, online journalists may make slightly higher salaries than their counterparts in traditional journalism. According to the U.S. Department of Labor, the median yearly income of traditional newspaper reporters was $32,270 in 2005. The lowest-paid 10 percent of all reporters earned less than $18,300; the highest-paid 10 percent earned more than $71,220. Online journalists generally earn salaries on the higher end of this scale. Salary.com reported that Web writers had salaries that ranged from less than $38,347 to $83,342 or more in 2007, depending on their level of expertise.

Incomes are influenced by such factors as the person's experience, company size, and geographic location. Freelance online journalists' hourly fees range from $25 to $125 depending on the project and the writer's experience.

Typical benefits may be available for full-time salaried employees, including sick leave, vacation pay, and health, life, and disability insurance. Retirement plans may also be available, and some companies may match employees' contributions. Some companies may also offer stock-option plans.

Freelance journalists do not receive benefits and are responsible for their own medical, disability, and life insurance. They do not receive vacation pay, and when they aren't working, they aren't generating income. Retirement plans must also be self-funded and self-directed.

WORK ENVIRONMENT

Online journalists may work in a variety of settings. Freelancers generally work out of their homes or private offices. Salaried writers working for a company generally work out of the company's offices in a clean, well-lit facility. Telecommuting is becoming more popular and may be an option at some companies. Whatever setting online journalists work in, they must have access to technology such as computers, modems, phones, and faxes.

Depending on the project, journalists may work independently or as part of a team of journalists. In addition, they frequently contact people outside of the journalism profession to interview for articles or information. Work hours may vary, and overtime may be needed to finish a project on deadline. Writing can be a frustrating job when articles do not come together as the writer had planned. The environment can be intense as journalists work to produce articles quickly while providing accurate and concise information.

Although publishing companies have traditionally had a business atmosphere, they are often more relaxed than other corporate environments. Many high-tech companies, especially smaller ones, also have a casual office atmosphere that promotes camaraderie and teamwork.

OUTLOOK

Though the overall employment rate for reporters is expected to grow slowly due to newspaper mergers, closures, decreased circulation, and more limited revenues, more rapid job growth is expected in new media areas, including online newspapers and magazines. The

Learn More about It

Bass, Frank. *The Associated Press Guide to Internet Research and Reporting.* New York: Perseus Publishing, 2002.

Craig, Richard. *Online Journalism: Reporting, Writing, and Editing for New Media.* Belmont, Calif.: Wadsworth Publishing, 2004.

Foust, James C. *Online Journalism: Principles and Practices of News for the Web.* Scottsdale, Ariz.: Holcomb Hathaway Publishing, 2004.

Hall, Jim. *Online Journalism: A Critical Primer.* London, U.K.: Pluto Press, 2001.

Hammerich, Irene, and Claire Harrison. *Developing Online Content: The Principles of Writing and Editing for the Web.* Hoboken, N.J.: John Wiley & Sons, 2001.

Pavlik, John Vernon, and Seymour Topping. *Journalism and New Media.* New York: Columbia University Press, 2001.

Ward, Mike. *Journalism Online.* Burlington, Mass.: Focal Press, 2002.

employment of online reporters should grow faster than the average for all occupations through the next decade. Traditional publishers and broadcasters have continued to move into Web publishing, indicating that online publishing will most likely continue to grow.

Online journalism will continue to evolve as journalists begin to devise new ways to take advantage of the interactivity offered by the Web. However, as the field becomes more established and the number of journalists who have online experience grows, competition for jobs is expected to become more intense.

The Internet and the Web publishing industry are relatively young, and job security with one company in the field is relatively low. Nevertheless, writers who are educated, keep up with technology, and continue to learn should not have problems finding employment.

FOR MORE INFORMATION

For ethics news and information on awards and internships, contact
Society of Professional Journalists
Eugene S. Pulliam National Journalism Center
3909 North Meridian Street
Indianapolis, IN 46208-4011
Tel: 317-927-8000
Email: hporter@spj.org
http://www.spj.org

For additional information regarding online writing and journalism, check out the following Web sites:
Contentious
http://www.contentious.com

Online News Association
PO Box 2022, Radio City Station
New York, NY 10101-2022
Tel: 646-290-7900
http://www.onlinenewsassociation.org

Visit the following Web site for comprehensive information on journalism careers, summer programs, and college journalism programs.
High School Journalism
http://www.highschooljournalism.org

To read an online magazine, check out this Web site.
Salon.com
http://www.salon.com

Press Secretaries and Political Consultants

QUICK FACTS

School Subjects
English
Government
Journalism

Personal Skills
Communication/ideas
Leadership/management

Work Environment
Primarily indoors
One location with some
travel

Minimum Education Level
Bachelor's degree

Salary Range
$26,870 to $45,020 to
$84,300+

Certification or Licensing
None available

Outlook
Faster than the average

DOT
168

GOE
N/A

NOC
N/A

O*NET-SOC
N/A

OVERVIEW

Press secretaries, political consultants, and other media relations professionals help politicians promote themselves and their issues among voters. They advise politicians on how to address the media. Sometimes called *spin doctors*, these professionals use the media to either change or strengthen public opinion. Press secretaries work for candidates and elected officials, while political consultants work with firms, contracting their services to politicians. The majority of press secretaries and political consultants work in Washington, D.C.; others work all across the country, involved with local and state government officials and candidates.

HISTORY

Using the media for political purposes is nearly as old as the U.S. government itself. The news media developed right alongside the political parties, and early newspapers served as a battleground for the Federalists and the Republicans. The first media moguls of the late 1800s often saw their newspapers as podiums from which to promote themselves. George Hearst bought the *San Francisco Examiner* in 1885 for the sole purpose of helping him campaign for Congress.

The latter half of the 20th century introduced whole other forms of media, which were quickly exploited by politicians seeking offices. Many historians mark the Kennedy-Nixon debate of 1960 as the moment when television coverage first became a key factor in the election process. Those who read of the

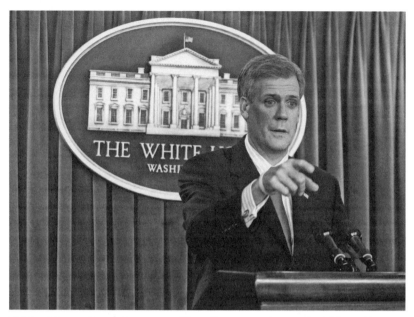

White House Press Secretary Tony Snow speaks to the White House press corps in the press briefing room of the White House. *(Corbis)*

debate in the next day's newspapers were under the impression that Nixon had easily won, but it was Kennedy's composure and appeal on camera that made the most powerful impression. Negative campaigning first showed its powerful influence in 1964, when Democratic presidential candidate Lyndon Johnson ran ads featuring a girl picking a flower while a nuclear bomb exploded in the background, which commented on Republican candidate Barry Goldwater's advocacy of strong military action in Vietnam.

Bill Clinton is just one president who benefited from the art of "spin," as his press secretaries and political managers were actively involved in dealing with his scandals and keeping his approval ratings high among the public. James Carville and George Stephanopoulos, working for Clinton's 1992 campaign, had the task of playing up Clinton's strengths as an intelligent, gifted politician, while down-playing negative associations. Their efforts were portrayed in the documentary *The War Room*, and their success earned them national renown as *spin doctors*.

THE JOB

If you were to manage a political campaign, how would you go about publicizing the candidate to the largest number of voters? You would use TV, of course. The need for TV and radio spots during a campaign is the reason running for office costs so much today. And it's also the reason many politicians hire professionals with an understanding of media relations to help them get elected. Once elected, a politician continues to rely on media relations experts, such as press secretaries, political consultants, and political managers, to use the media to portray the politician in the best light. In recent years, such words as *spin*, *leak*, and *sound bite* have entered the daily vocabulary of news and politics to describe elements of political coverage in the media.

Political consultants usually work independently, or as members of consulting firms, and contract with individuals. Political consultants are involved in producing radio and TV ads, writing campaign plans, and developing themes for these campaigns. A theme may focus on a specific issue or on the differences between the client and the opponent. Their client may be new to the political arena or someone established looking to maintain an office. They conduct polls and surveys to gauge public opinion and to identify their client's biggest competition. Political consultants advise their clients in the best ways to use the media. In addition to TV and radio, the Internet has proven important to politicians. Consultants launch campaign Web sites and also chase down rumors that spread across the Internet. A consultant may be hired for an entire campaign, or may be hired only to produce an ad, or to come up with a sound bite (or catchy quote) for the media.

Though voters across the country complain about negative campaigning, or "mud-slinging," such campaigns have proven effective. In his 1988 presidential campaign, George Bush ran TV ads featuring the now notorious Willie Horton, a convict who was released from prison only to commit another crime. The ad was intended to suggest that his opponent had a soft approach to crime. It proved very effective in undermining the campaign of Michael Dukakis and putting him on the defensive. Many consultants believe they must focus on a few specific issues in a campaign, emphasizing their client's strengths as well as the opponent's weaknesses.

Press secretaries serve on the congressional staffs of senators and representatives and on the staffs of governors and mayors. The president also has a press secretary. Press secretaries and their assistants write press releases and opinion pieces to publicize the efforts of the government officials for whom they work. They also help prepare speeches and prepare their employers for press conferences and interviews. They maintain Web sites, posting press releases and the results of press conferences.

Media relations experts are often called spin doctors because of their ability to manipulate the media, or put a good spin on a news story to best suit the purposes of their clients. Corporations also rely on spin for positive media coverage. Media relations experts are often called upon during a political scandal, or after corporate blunders, for damage control. Using the newspapers and radio and TV broadcasts, spin doctors attempt to downplay public relations disasters, helping politicians and corporations save face. In highly sensitive situations, they must answer questions selectively and carefully, and they may even be involved in secretly releasing, or leaking, information to the press. Because of these manipulations, media relations professionals are often disrespected. They're sometimes viewed as people who conceal facts and present lies, prey on the emotions of voters, or even represent companies responsible for illegal practices. However, many political consultants and media representatives are responsible for bringing public attention to important issues and good political candidates. They also help organizations and nonprofit groups advocate for legislative issues and help develop support for school funding, environmental concerns, and other community needs.

REQUIREMENTS

High School
English composition, drama, and speech classes will help you develop good communication skills, while government, history, and civics classes will teach you about the structure of local, state, and federal government. Take math, economics, and accounting courses to prepare for poll-taking and for analyzing statistics and demographics.

While in high school, work with your school newspaper, radio station, or TV station. This will help you recognize how important reporters, editors, and producers are in putting together newspapers and shaping news segments. You should also consider joining your school's speech and debate team to gain experience in research and in making persuasive arguments.

Postsecondary Training
Most people in media relations have bachelor's degrees, and some also hold master's degrees, doctorates, and law degrees. As an undergraduate, you should enroll in a four-year college and pursue a well-rounded education. Press secretaries and political consultants need a good understanding of the history and culture of the United States and foreign countries. Some of the majors you should consider as an undergraduate include journalism, political science, English, marketing, and economics. You should take courses in government, psychology, statistics, history, and a foreign language. You might then choose to pursue a graduate degree in journalism, political science, public administration, or international relations.

Seek a college with a good internship program. You might also pursue internships with local and state officials and your congressional members in the Senate and House of Representatives. Journalism internships will involve you with local and national publications, or the news departments of radio and TV stations.

Other Requirements

In this career, you need to be very organized and capable of juggling many different tasks, from quickly writing ads and press releases to developing budgets and expense accounts. You need good problem-solving skills and some imagination when putting a positive spin on negative issues. Good people skills are important so that you can develop contacts within government and the media. You should feel comfortable with public speaking, leading press conferences, and speaking on behalf of your employers and clients. You should also enjoy competition. You can't be intimidated by people in power or by journalists questioning the issues addressed in your campaigns.

EXPLORING

Get involved with your school government as well as with committees and clubs that have officers and elections. You can also become involved in local, state, and federal elections by volunteering for campaigns; though you may just be making phone calls and putting up signs, you may also have the opportunity to write press releases and schedule press conferences and interviews, and you will see first-hand how a campaign operates.

Working for your school newspaper will help you learn about conducting research, interviews, and opinion polls, which all play a part in managing media relations. You may be able to get a part-time job or an internship with your city's newspaper or broadcast news station, where you will gain experience with election coverage and political advertising. Visit the Web sites of U.S. Congress members. Many sites feature lists of recent press releases, which will give you a sense of how a press office publicizes the efforts and actions of Congress members. Read some of the many books examining recent political campaigns and scandals, and read magazines like *Harper's* (http://www.harpers.org), *The Atlantic* (http://www.theatlantic.com), and the online magazine *Salon.com* (http://www.salon.com) for political commentary.

EMPLOYERS

Though a majority of press secretaries and political consultants work in Washington, D.C., others work in state capitals and major cities all across the country. Press secretaries work for local, state, and federal government officials. They also find work with public relations agencies, and the press offices of large corporations. Celebrities, and others in the public eye also hire press agents to help them control rumors and publicity.

Political consultants are generally self-employed, or work for consulting firms that specialize in media relations. They contract with politicians, corporations, nonprofit groups, and trade and professional associations. They participate in the campaigns of mayors, governors, and Congress members as well as in the political campaigns of other countries.

STARTING OUT

Media relations jobs are rarely advertised, and there is no predetermined path to success. It is recommended that you make connections with people in both politics and the media. Volunteer for political campaigns, and also advocate for public policy issues of interest to you. You can make good connections, and gain valuable experience, working or interning in the offices of your state capital. You might

Learn More About It

Faucheux, Ron. *Running for Office: The Strategies, Techniques, and Messages Modern Political Candidates Need to Win Elections.* New York: M. Evans and Company, 2002.

Guzzetta, S. J. *The Campaign Manual: A Definitive Study of the Modern Political Campaign Process.* 7th ed. Flat Rock, N.C.: Political Publications, 2006.

Johnson, Dennis W. *No Place for Amateurs: How Political Consultants Are Reshaping American Democracy.* 2d ed. New York: Routledge, 2007.

Nash, Phil Tajitsu, and Emilienne Ireland. *Winning Campaigns Online: Strategies for Candidates and Causes.* 2d ed. Bethesda, MD: Science Writers Press, 2001.

Patterson, Bradley H., Jr. *The White House Staff: Inside the West Wing and Beyond.* Revised ed. Washington, D.C.: Brookings Institution Press, 2002.

Shea, Daniel M., and Michael John Burton. *Campaign Craft: The Strategies, Tactics, and Art of Political Campaign Management.* 3d ed. Westport, Conn.: Praeger Paperback, 2006.

Thurber, James A. *Campaign Warriors: Political Consultants in Elections.* Washington, D.C.: Brookings Institution Press, 2000.

also try for an internship with one of your state's members of Congress; contact their offices in Washington, D.C. for internship applications. If you're more interested in the writing and producing aspects of the career, work for local newspapers or the broadcast news media; or work as a producer for a television production crew or for an ad agency that specializes in political campaigns. A political consulting firm may hire assistants for writing and for commercial production. Whereas some people pursue the career directly by working in the press offices of political candidates, others find their way into political consulting after having worked as lawyers, lobbyists, or journalists.

ADVANCEMENT

A press secretary who has worked closely with a successful government official may advance into a higher staff position, like chief of staff or legislative director. Political consultants, after winning many elections and establishing credentials, will begin to take on more prominent clients and major campaigns. Network TV, cable, and radio news departments also hire successful media relations experts to serve as political analysts on the air. Some consultants also write columns for newspapers and syndicates and publish books about their insights into politics.

EARNINGS

According to the U.S. Department of Labor, public relations specialists (which includes press secretaries) had median annual earnings of $45,020 in 2005, with salaries ranging from less than $26,870 to more than $84,300. In 2005, median earnings for those who worked in local government were $48,460; state government, $64,198; and federal government, $72,600.

The incomes of political consultants vary greatly. Someone contracting with local candidates, or with state organizations and associations, may make around $40,000 a year; someone consulting with high-profile candidates may earn hundreds of thousands of dollars a year.

WORK ENVIRONMENT

Representing politicians can be thankless work. Press secretaries may have to speak to the press about sensitive, volatile issues and deal directly with the frustrations of journalists unable to get the answers they want. When working for prominent politicians, they may become the subject of personal attacks.

Despite these potential conflicts, the work can be exciting and fast-paced. Press secretaries and political consultants see the results of their efforts in the newspapers and on television, and they have the satisfaction of influencing voters and public opinion. If working on a campaign as a consultant, their hours will be long and stressful. In some cases, they will have to scrap unproductive media ads and start from scratch with only hours to write, produce, and place new commercials. They will also have to be available to their clients around the clock, especially as an election draws near.

OUTLOOK

Employment for public relations specialists, which includes press secretaries and political consultants, is expected to grow faster than the average through 2014. Consultants and media representatives will become increasingly important to candidates and elected officials. Television ads and Internet campaigns have become almost necessary to reach the public. The work of press secretaries will expand as more news networks and news magazines closely follow the decisions and actions of government officials.

The Pew Research Center, which surveys public opinion on political issues, has found that most Americans are concerned about negative campaigning, while most political consultants see nothing wrong with using negative tactics in advertising. Despite how the general public may feel about negative campaigning, it remains a very effective political tool. In some local elections, candidates may mutually agree to avoid the mudslinging, but the use of negative ads in general is likely to increase.

Campaigning will continue to be affected by developing technology. Voters are now able to access more information about candidates and issues via the Internet. As political blogs and other sources of information for voters become increasingly important, press secretaries and political consultants will need to devote more effort to using these emerging media. Also, the increase in the number of channels available to cable TV viewers makes it more difficult for candidates to advertise to a general audience. However, the greater number of outlets for media products will create an increased demand for writers, TV producers, and Web designers to help candidates reach potential voters.

FOR MORE INFORMATION

This organization provides professional guidance, assistance, and education to members and maintains a code of ethics.
American Association of Political Consultants
600 Pennsylvania Avenue, SE, Suite 330

Washington, DC 20003-6300
Tel: 202-544-9815
Email: info@theaapc.org
http://www.theaapc.org

For general information about careers in broadcast media, contact
National Association of Broadcasters
1771 N Street, NW
Washington, DC 20036-2800
Tel: 202-429-5300
Email: nab@nab.org
http://www.nab.org

Visit the Web sites of the House and the Senate for press releases and links to sites for individual members of Congress. To write to your state representatives, contact
Office of Senator (Name)
United States Senate
Washington, DC 20510-0001
http://www.senate.gov

Office of Congressperson (Name)
U.S. House of Representatives
Washington, DC 20515-0001
http://www.house.gov

The Pew Research Center is an opinion research group that studies attitudes toward press, politics, and public policy issues. To read some of their survey results, visit its Web site or contact
The Pew Research Center for the People and the Press
1615 L Street, NW, Suite 700
Washington, DC 20036-5621
Tel: 202-419-4350
Email: info@people-press.org
http://people-press.org

Public Relations Specialists

OVERVIEW

Public relations (PR) specialists develop and maintain programs that present a favorable public image for an individual or organization. They provide information to the target audience (generally, the public at large) about the client, its goals and accomplishments, and any further plans or projects that may be of public interest.

PR specialists may be employed by corporations, government agencies, nonprofit organizations, or almost any type of organization. Many PR specialists hold positions in public relations consulting firms or work for advertising agencies. There are approximately 188,000 public relations specialists in the United States.

HISTORY

The first public relations counsel was a reporter named Ivy Ledbetter Lee, who in 1906 was named press representative for a group of coalmine operators. Labor disputes were becoming a large concern of the operators, and they had run into problems because of their continual refusal to talk to the press and the hired miners. Lee convinced the mine operators to start responding to press questions and supply the press with information on the mine activities.

During and after World War II, the rapid advancement of communications techniques prompted firms to realize they needed professional help to ensure their messages were given proper public attention. Manufacturing firms that had turned their production

Museum of Public Relations

In late 1997, Spector & Associates debuted the Museum of Public Relations on the Internet. The museum is meant to provide a history and examples of successful public relations programs for industry, education, and government, using photographs and stories. Read about such public relations trendsetters as Edward L. Bernays, Moss Kendrix, Carl R. Byoir, Arthur W. Page, and Chester Burger. For more information, visit http://www.prmuseum.com.

facilities over to the war effort returned to the manufacture of peacetime products and enlisted the aid of public relations professionals to forcefully and convincingly bring products and the company name before the buying public.

Large business firms, labor unions, and service organizations, such as the American Red Cross, Boy Scouts of America, and the YMCA, began to recognize the value of establishing positive, healthy relationships with the public that they served and depended on for support. The need for effective public relations was often emphasized when circumstances beyond a company's or institution's control created unfavorable reactions from the public.

Public relations specialists must be experts at representing their clients before the media. The rapid growth of the public relations field since 1945 is testimony to the increased awareness in all industries of the need for professional attention to the proper use of media and the proper public relations approach to the many publics of a firm or an organization—customers, employees, stockholders, contributors, and competitors.

THE JOB

Public relations specialists are employed to do a variety of tasks. They may be employed primarily as writers, creating reports, news releases, and booklet texts. Others write speeches or create copy for radio, TV, or film sequences. These workers often spend much of their time contacting the press, radio, and TV as well as magazines on behalf of the employer. Some PR specialists work more as editors than writers, fact-checking and rewriting employee publications, newsletters, shareholder reports, and other management communications.

Specialists may choose to concentrate in graphic design, using their background knowledge of art and layout for developing brochures, booklets, and photographic communications. Other PR workers handle special events, such as press parties, convention exhibits, open houses, or anniversary celebrations.

PR specialists must be alert to any and all company or institutional events that are newsworthy. They prepare news releases and direct them toward the proper media. Specialists working for manufacturers and retailers are concerned with efforts that will promote sales and create goodwill for the firm's products. They work closely with the marketing and sales departments in announcing new products, preparing displays, and attending occasional dealers' conventions.

A large firm may have a *director of public relations* who is a vice president of the company and in charge of a staff that includes writers, artists, researchers, and other specialists. Publicity for an individual or a small organization may involve many of the same areas of expertise but may be carried out by a few people or possibly even one person.

Many PR workers act as consultants (rather than staff) of a corporation, association, college, hospital, or other institution. These workers have the advantage of being able to operate independently, state opinions objectively, and work with more than one type of business or association.

PR specialists are called upon to work with the public opinion aspects of almost every corporate or institutional problem. These can range from the opening of a new manufacturing plant to a college's dormitory dedication to a merger or sale of a company.

Public relations professionals may specialize. *Lobbyists* try to persuade legislators and other office holders to pass laws favoring the interests of the firms or people they represent. *Fund-raising directors* develop and direct programs designed to raise funds for social welfare agencies and other nonprofit organizations.

Early in their careers, public relations specialists become accustomed to having others receive credit for their behind-the-scenes work. The speeches they draft will be delivered by company officers, the magazine articles they prepare may be credited to the president of the company, and they may be consulted to prepare the message to stockholders from the chairman of the board that appears in the annual report.

REQUIREMENTS

High School

While in high school, take courses in English, journalism, public speaking, humanities, and languages because public relations is based on effective communication with others. Courses such as these will develop your skills in written and oral communication as well as provide a better understanding of different fields and industries to be publicized.

Postsecondary Training

Most people employed in public relations service have a college degree. Major fields of study most beneficial to developing the proper skills are public relations, English, and journalism. Some employers feel that majoring in the area in which the public relations person will eventually work is the best training. A knowledge of business administration is most helpful as is a native talent for selling. A graduate degree may be required for managerial positions. People with a bachelor's degree in public relations can find staff positions with either an organization or a public relations firm.

More than 200 colleges and about 100 graduate schools offer degree programs or special courses in public relations. In addition, many other colleges offer at least courses in the field. Public relations programs are sometimes administered by the journalism or communication departments of schools. In addition to courses in theory and techniques of public relations, interested individuals may study organization, management and administration, and practical applications and often specialize in areas such as business, government, and nonprofit organizations. Other preparation includes courses in creative writing, psychology, communications, advertising, and journalism.

Certification or Licensing

The Public Relations Society of America and the International Association of Business Communicators accredit public relations workers who have at least five years of experience in the field and pass a comprehensive examination. Such accreditation is a sign of competence in this field, although it is not a requirement for employment.

Other Requirements

Today's public relations specialist must be a businessperson first, both to understand how to perform successfully in business and to comprehend the needs and goals of the organization or client. Additionally, the public relations specialist needs to be a strong writer and speaker, with good interpersonal, leadership, and organizational skills.

EXPLORING

Almost any experience in working with other people will help you to develop strong interpersonal skills, which are crucial in public

Get Advice from a Mentor

The Public Relations Society of America (PRSA) has a College of Fellows Mentoring program that allows participants to receive career advice from accredited professionals with 20 years or more of experience. The College of Fellows is a group of PR experts elected to the College because they "demonstrate superior capability as a practitioner, exhibit personal and professional qualities that serve as a role model for other practitioners, and have advanced the state of the profession." They offer their business knowledge to individuals who are considering changing jobs, trying to advance into a management position, or facing other professional challenges. You can register for the service online (free for PRSA members, $110 for nonmembers) and you will be matched with a College of Fellows member who has volunteered to consult on the topic you need help with. For information, see the Professional Development section of the PRSA Web site at http://www.prsa.org.

relations. The possibilities are almost endless. Summer work on a newspaper or trade paper or with a radio or television station may give insight into communications media. Working as a volunteer on a political campaign can help you to understand the ways in which people can be persuaded. Being selected as a page for the U.S. Congress or a state legislature will help you grasp the fundamentals of government processes. A job in retail will help you to understand some of the principles of product presentation. A teaching job will develop your organization and presentation skills. These are just some of the jobs that will let you explore areas of public relations.

EMPLOYERS

Public relations specialists hold about 188,000 jobs. Workers may be paid employees of the organization they represent or they may be part of a public relations firm that works for organizations on a contract basis. Others are involved in fund-raising or political campaigning. Public relations may be done for a corporation, retail business, service company, utility, association, nonprofit organization, or educational institution.

Most PR firms are located in large cities that are centers of communications. New York, Chicago, San Francisco, Los Angeles, and Washington, D.C., are good places to start a search for a public relations job. Nevertheless, there are many good opportunities in cities across the United States.

STARTING OUT

There is no clear-cut formula for getting a job in public relations. Individuals often enter the field after gaining preliminary experience in another occupation closely allied to the field, usually some segment of communications, and frequently, in journalism. Coming into public relations from newspaper work is still a recommended route. Another good method is to gain initial employment as a public relations trainee or intern, or as a clerk, secretary, or research assistant in a public relations department or a counseling firm.

ADVANCEMENT

In some large companies, an entry-level public relations specialist may start as a trainee in a formal training program for new employees. In others, new employees may expect to be assigned to work that has a minimum of responsibility. They may assemble clippings or do rewrites on material that has already been accepted. They may make posters or assist in conducting polls or surveys, or compile reports from data submitted by others.

As workers acquire experience, they are typically given more responsibility. They write news releases, direct polls or surveys, or advance to writing speeches for company officials. Progress may seem to be slow, because some skills take a long time to master.

Some advance in responsibility and salary in the same firm in which they started. Others find that the path to advancement is to accept a more rewarding position in another firm.

The goal of many public relations specialists is to open an independent office or to join an established consulting firm. To start an independent office requires a large outlay of capital and an established reputation in the field. However, those who are successful in operating their own consulting firms probably attain the greatest financial success in the public relations field.

EARNINGS

Public relations specialists had median annual earnings of $45,020 in 2005, according to the U.S. Department of Labor. Salaries ranged from less than $26,870 to more than $84,300. The department reports the following 2005 median salaries for public relations specialists by type of employer: advertising and related services, $57,160; professional and similar organizations, $55,470; colleges and universities, $44,420; and local government, $48,460.

Many PR workers receive a range of fringe benefits from corporations and agencies employing them, including bonus/incentive compensation, stock options, profit sharing/pension plans/401(k) programs, medical benefits, life insurance, financial planning, maternity/paternity leave, paid vacations, and family college tuition. Bonuses can range from 5 to 100 percent of base compensation and often are based on individual and/or company performance.

WORK ENVIRONMENT

Public relations specialists generally work in offices with adequate secretarial help, regular salary increases, and expense accounts. They are expected to make a good appearance in tasteful, conservative clothing. They must have social poise, and their conduct in their personal life is important to their firms or their clients. The public relations specialist may have to entertain business associates.

The PR specialist seldom works conventional office hours for many weeks at a time; although the workweek may consist of 35 to 40 hours, these hours may be supplemented by evenings and even weekends when meetings must be attended and other special events covered. Time behind the desk may represent only a small part of the total working schedule. Travel is often an important and necessary part of the job.

The life of the PR worker is so greatly determined by the job that many consider this a disadvantage. Because the work is concerned with public opinion, it is often difficult to measure the results of performance and to sell the worth of a public relations program to an employer or client. Competition in the consulting field is keen, and if a firm loses an account, some of its personnel may be affected. The demands it makes for anonymity will be considered by some as one of the profession's less inviting aspects. Public relations involves much more hard work and a great deal less glamour than is popularly supposed.

OUTLOOK

Employment of public relations professionals is expected to grow faster than average for all other occupations through 2014, according to the U.S. Department of Labor. Competition will be keen for beginning jobs in public relations because so many job seekers are enticed by the perceived glamour and appeal of the field; those with both education and experience will have an advantage.

Most large companies have some sort of public relations resource, either through their own staff or through the use of a firm of consultants. Most are expected to expand their public relations activities, creating many new jobs. More smaller companies are hiring public relations specialists, adding to the demand for these workers. Additionally, as a result of recent corporate scandals, more public relations specialists will be hired to help improve the images of companies and regain the trust of the public.

FOR MORE INFORMATION

For information on accreditation, contact
International Association of Business Communicators
One Hallidie Plaza, Suite 600
San Francisco, CA 94102-2818
Tel: 415-544-4700
http://www.iabc.com

For statistics, salary surveys, and information on accreditation and student membership, contact
Public Relations Society of America
33 Maiden Lane, 11th Floor
New York, NY 10038-5150
Tel: 212-460-1466
Email: prssa@prsa.org (student membership)
http://www.prsa.org

This professional association for public relations professionals offers an accreditation program and opportunities for professional development.
Canadian Public Relations Society Inc.
4195 Dundas Street West, Suite 346
Toronto, ON M8X 1Y4 Canada
Tel: 416-239-7034
Email: admin@cprs.ca
http://www.cprs.ca

Reporters

OVERVIEW

Reporters are the foot soldiers for newspapers, magazines, and television and radio broadcast companies. They gather and analyze information about current events and write stories for publication or for broadcasting. *News analysts*, *reporters*, and *correspondents* hold about 64,000 jobs in the United States.

HISTORY

Newspapers are the primary disseminators of news in the United States. People read newspapers to learn about the current events that are shaping their society and societies around the world. Newspapers give public expression to opinion and criticism of government and societal issues, and, of course, provide the public with entertaining, informative reading.

Newspapers are able to fulfill these functions because of the freedom given to the press. However, this was not always the case. The first American newspaper, published in 1690, was suppressed four days after it was published. And it was not until 1704 that the first continuous newspaper appeared in the American colonies.

One early newspaperman who later became a famous writer was Benjamin Franklin. Franklin worked for his brother at a Boston newspaper before publishing his own paper two years later in 1723 in Philadelphia.

A number of developments in the printing industry made it possible for newspapers to be printed more cheaply. In the late 19th century, new types of presses were developed to increase production,

A television reporter covers the 2000 presidential recount in West Palm Beach, FL. *(Photo Researchers)*

and more importantly, the Linotype machine was invented. The Linotype mechanically set letters so that handset type was no longer necessary. This dramatically decreased the amount of prepress time needed to get a page into print. Newspapers could respond to breaking stories more quickly, and late editions with breaking stories became part of the news world.

These technological advances, along with an increasing population, factored into the rapid growth of the newspaper industry in the United States. In 1776, there were only 37 newspapers in the United States. Today there are about 1,500 daily and nearly 7,500 weekly newspapers in the country.

As newspapers grew in size and widened the scope of their coverage, it became necessary to increase the number of employees and to assign them specialized jobs. Reporters have always been the heart of newspaper staffs. However, in today's complex world, with the public hungry for news as it occurs, reporters and correspondents are involved in all media—not only newspapers, but magazines, radio, and television as well. Today, many newspapers are available in both online and print versions.

THE JOB

Reporters collect information on newsworthy events and prepare stories for newspaper or magazine publication or for radio or television broadcast. The stories may simply provide information about local, state, or national events, or they may present opposing points of view on issues of current interest. In this latter capacity, the press plays an important role in monitoring the actions of public officials and others in positions of power.

Stories may originate as an assignment from an editor or as the result of a lead, or news tip. Good reporters are always on the lookout for good story ideas. To cover a story, they gather and verify facts by interviewing people involved in or related to the event, examining documents and public records, observing events as they happen, and researching relevant background information. Reporters generally take notes or use a tape recorder as they collect information and write their stories once they return to their offices. In order to meet a deadline, they may have to telephone the stories to rewriters, who write or transcribe the stories for them. After the facts have been gathered and verified, the reporters transcribe their notes, organize their material, and determine what emphasis, or angle, to give the news. The story is then written to meet prescribed standards of editorial style and format.

The basic functions of reporters are to observe events objectively and impartially, record them accurately, and explain what the news means in a larger, societal context. Within this framework, there are several types of reporters.

The most basic is the *news reporter.* This job sometimes involves covering a beat, which means that the reporter may be assigned to consistently cover news from an area such as the local courthouse, police station, or school system. It may involve receiving general assignments, such as a story about an unusual occurrence or an obituary of a community leader. Large daily papers may assign teams of reporters to investigate social, economic, or political events and conditions.

Many newspaper, wire service, and magazine reporters specialize in one type of story, either because they have a particular interest in the subject or because they have acquired the expertise to analyze and interpret news in that particular area. *Topical reporters* cover stories for a specific department, such as medicine, politics, foreign affairs, sports, consumer affairs, finance, science, business, education, labor, or religion. They sometimes write features explaining the history that has led up to certain events in the field they cover. *Feature writers* generally write longer, broader stories than news reporters, usually on more upbeat subjects, such as fashion, art, theater, travel, and social events. They may write about trends, for example, or profile local celebrities. *Editorial writers* and *syndicated news columnists* present viewpoints that, although based on a thorough knowledge, are opinions on topics of popular interest. Columnists write under a byline and usually specialize in a particular subject, such as politics or government activities. *Critics* review restaurants, books, works of art, movies, plays, musical performances, and other cultural events.

Specializing allows reporters to focus their efforts, talent, and knowledge on one area of expertise. It also gives them more opportunities to develop deeper relationships with contacts and sources, which is necessary to gain access to the news.

Correspondents report events in locations distant from their home offices. They may report news by mail, telephone, fax, or computer from rural areas, large cities throughout the United States, or countries. Many large newspapers, magazines, and broadcast companies have one correspondent who is responsible for covering all the news for the foreign city or country where they are based. These reporters are known as *foreign correspondents*.

Reporters on small or weekly newspapers not only cover all aspects of the news in their communities, but also may take photographs, write editorials and headlines, layout pages, edit wire-service copy, and help with general office work. Television reporters may have to be photogenic as well as talented and resourceful: They may at times present live reports, filmed by a mobile camera unit at the scene where the news originates, or they may tape interviews and narration for later broadcast.

REQUIREMENTS

High School
High school courses that will provide you with a firm foundation for a reporting career include English, journalism, history, social studies, communications, typing, and computer science. Speech courses will help you hone your interviewing skills, which are necessary for success as a reporter. In addition, it will be helpful to take college prep courses, such as foreign languages, math, and science.

Postsecondary Training
You will need at least a bachelor's degree to become a reporter, and a graduate degree will give you a great advantage over those entering the field with lesser degrees. Most editors prefer applicants with degrees in journalism because their studies include liberal arts courses as well as professional training in journalism. Some editors consider it sufficient for a reporter to have a good general education from a liberal

arts college. Others prefer applicants with an undergraduate degree in liberal arts and a master's degree in journalism. The great majority of journalism graduates hired today by newspapers, wire services, and magazines have majored specifically in news-editorial journalism.

More than 1,200 institutions offer programs in journalism or communication, or related programs. More than 400 colleges offer programs in journalism leading to a bachelor's degree. In these schools, around three-fourths of a student's time is devoted to a liberal arts education and one-fourth to the professional study of journalism, with required courses such as introductory mass media, basic reporting and copyediting, history of journalism, and press law and ethics. Students are encouraged to select other journalism courses according to their specific interests.

Journalism courses and programs are also offered by many community and junior colleges. Graduates of these programs are prepared to go to work directly as general assignment reporters, but they may encounter difficulty when competing with graduates of four-year programs. Credit earned in community and junior colleges may be transferable to four-year programs in journalism at other colleges and universities. Journalism training may also be obtained in the armed forces. Names and addresses of newspapers and a list of journalism schools and departments are published in the annual *Editor & Publisher International Year Book: The Encyclopedia of the Newspaper Industry* (New York: Editor & Publisher, 2006), which is available for reference in most public libraries and newspaper offices.

A master's degree in journalism may be earned at approximately 120 schools, and a doctorate at about 35 schools. Graduate degrees may prepare students specifically for careers in news or as journalism teachers, researchers, and theorists, or for jobs in advertising or public relations.

A reporter's liberal arts training should include courses in English (with an emphasis on writing), sociology, political science, economics, history, psychology, business, speech, and computer science. Knowledge of foreign languages is also useful. To be a reporter in a specialized field, such as science or finance, requires concentrated course work in that area.

Other Requirements

In order to succeed as a reporter, it is crucial that you have good typing skills, since you will type your stories using word processing programs. Although not essential, knowledge of shorthand or speedwriting makes note taking easier, and familiarity with news photography is an asset.

You must also be inquisitive, aggressive, persistent, and detail-oriented. You should enjoy interaction with people of various races, cultures, religions, economic levels, and social statuses.

EXPLORING

You can explore a career as a reporter in a number of ways. You can talk to reporters and editors at local newspapers and radio and TV stations. You can interview the admissions counselor at the school of journalism closest to your home.

In addition to taking courses in English, journalism, social studies, speech, computer science, and typing, high school students can acquire practical experience by working on school newspapers or on a church, synagogue, or mosque newsletter. Part-time and summer jobs on newspapers provide invaluable experience to the aspiring reporter.

College students can develop their reporting skills in the laboratory courses or workshops that are part of the journalism curriculum. College students might also accept jobs as campus correspondents for selected newspapers. People who work as part-time reporters covering news in a particular area of a community are known as stringers and are paid only for those stories that are printed.

More than 3,000 journalism scholarships, fellowships, and assistantships are offered by universities, newspapers, foundations, and professional organizations to college students. Many newspapers and magazines offer summer internships to journalism students to provide them with practical experience in a variety of basic reporting and editing duties. Students who successfully complete internships are usually placed in jobs more quickly upon graduation than those without such experience.

EMPLOYERS

Of the approximately 64,000 reporters and correspondents employed in the United States, nearly 61 percent work for newspapers, periodical, book, and directory publishers. About 25 percent work in radio and television broadcasting. About 7 percent are self-employed, working on a project or freelance basis or on their own publications and broadcasts.

STARTING OUT

Jobs in this field may be obtained through college placement offices or by applying directly to the personnel departments of individual employers. If you have some practical experience, you will have an advantage;

you should be prepared to present a portfolio of material you wrote as a volunteer or part-time reporter, or other writing samples.

Most journalism school graduates start out as general assignment reporters or copy editors for small publications. A few outstanding journalism graduates may be hired by large city newspapers or national magazines. They are trained on the job. But they are the exception, as large employers usually require several years' experience. As a rule, novice reporters cover routine assignments, such as reporting on civic and club meetings, writing obituaries, or summarizing speeches. As you become more skilled in reporting, you will be assigned to more important events or to a regular beat, or you may specialize in a particular field.

ADVANCEMENT

Reporters may advance by moving to larger newspapers or press services, but competition for such positions is unusually keen. Many highly qualified reporters apply for these jobs every year.

A select number of reporters eventually become columnists, correspondents, editorial writers, editors, or top executives. These important and influential positions represent the top of the field, and competition is strong for them.

Many reporters transfer the contacts and knowledge developed in newspaper reporting to related fields, such as public relations, advertising, or preparing copy for radio and television news programs.

EARNINGS

There are great variations in the earnings of reporters. Salaries are related to experience, the type of employer for which the reporter works, geographic location, and whether the reporter is covered by a contract negotiated by the Newspaper Guild.

According to the National Occupational Employment and Wage Estimates, a salary survey by the U.S. Department of Labor, the median salary for news analysts, reporters, and correspondents was $32,270 in 2005. The lowest-paid 10 percent of these workers earned $18,300 or less per year, while the highest-paid 10 percent made $71,220 or more annually.

According to the Newspaper Guild, the average top minimum salary for reporters with about five years' experience was $44,580 in 2003. Salaries range from $20,000 to $65,000 or more.

The U.S. Department of Labor reported that news analysts who worked in radio and television broadcasting had median annual earnings of $42,810 in 2005.

WORK ENVIRONMENT

Reporters work under a great deal of pressure in settings that differ from the typical business office. Their jobs generally require a five-day, 35- to 40-hour week, but overtime and irregular schedules are very common. Reporters employed by morning papers start work in the late afternoon and finish around midnight, while those on afternoon or evening papers start early in the morning and work until early or mid-afternoon. Foreign correspondents often work late at night to send the news to their papers in time to meet printing deadlines.

The day of the smoky, ink-stained newsroom has passed, but newspaper offices remain hectic places. Reporters have to work amid the clatter of computer keyboards and other machines, loud voices engaged in telephone conversations, and the bustle created by people hurrying about. An atmosphere of excitement prevails, especially as press deadlines approach.

Travel is often required in this occupation, and some assignments may be dangerous, such as covering wars, political uprisings, fires, floods, and other events of a volatile nature.

OUTLOOK

Employment for reporters and correspondents through 2014 is expected to grow more slowly than the average for all occupations, according to the *Occupational Outlook Handbook*. While the number of self-employed reporters and correspondents is expected to grow, newspaper jobs are expected to decrease because of mergers, consolidations, and closures in the newspaper industry.

Because of an increase in the number of small community and suburban daily and weekly newspapers, opportunities will be best for journalism graduates who are willing to relocate and accept relatively low starting salaries. With experience, reporters on these small papers can move up to editing positions or may choose to transfer to reporting jobs on larger newspapers or magazines.

Openings will be limited on big city dailies. While individual papers may enlarge their reporting staffs, little or no change is expected in the total number of these newspapers. Applicants will face strong competition for jobs on large metropolitan newspapers. Experience is a definite requirement, which rules out most new graduates unless they possess credentials in an area for which the publication has a pressing need. Occasionally, a beginner can use contacts and experience gained through internship programs and summer jobs to obtain a reporting job immediately after graduation.

A significant number of jobs will be provided by magazines and in radio and television broadcasting, but the major news magazines and larger broadcasting stations generally prefer experienced reporters. For beginning correspondents, small stations with local news broadcasts will continue to replace staff who move on to larger stations or leave the business. Network hiring has been cut drastically in the past few years and will probably continue to decline.

Stronger employment growth is expected for reporters in online newspapers and magazines, given the increasing importance of online news sources.

Overall, the prospects are best for graduates who have majored in news-editorial journalism and completed an internship while in school. The top graduates in an accredited program will have a great advantage, as will talented technical and scientific writers. Small newspapers prefer to hire beginning reporters who are acquainted with the community and are willing to help with photography and other aspects of production. Without at least a bachelor's degree in journalism, applicants will find it increasingly difficult to obtain even an entry-level position.

Those with doctorates and practical reporting experience may find teaching positions at four-year colleges and universities, while highly qualified reporters with master's degrees may obtain employment in journalism departments of community and junior colleges.

Poor economic conditions do not drastically affect the employment of reporters and correspondents. Their numbers are not severely cut back even during a downturn; instead, employers forced to reduce expenditures will suspend new hiring.

FOR MORE INFORMATION

This organization provides general educational information on all areas of journalism, including newspapers, magazines, television, and radio.

Association for Education in Journalism and Mass Communication
234 Outlet Pointe Boulevard
Columbia, SC 29210-5667
Tel: 803-798-0271
http://www.aejmc.org

To receive a copy of The Journalist's Road to Success, *which lists schools offering degrees in news-editorial and financial aid to those interested in print journalism, contact*

Dow Jones Newspaper Fund
PO Box 300
Princeton, NJ 08543-0300

Tel: 609-452-2820
Email: newsfund@wsj.dowjones.com
http://djnewspaperfund.dowjones.com/fund

For information on careers in newspapers and industry facts and figures, contact
Newspaper Association of America
4401 Wilson Boulevard, Suite 900
Arlington, VA 22203-1867
Tel: 571-366-1000
Email: IRC@naa.org
http://www.naa.org

For information on union membership, contact
Newspaper Guild-Communication Workers of America
501 Third Street, NW
Washington, DC 20001-2797
Tel: 202-434-7177
http://www.newsguild.org

INTERVIEW

Meg Heckman is a staff writer for the Concord Monitor *in Concord, New Hampshire. She was recently named Writer of the Year by the New Hampshire Press Association and Community Reporter of the Year by the New England Society of Newspaper Editors. She spoke with the editors of* Careers in Focus: Writing *about her professional experience and the field of reporting in general.*

Q. What are the main responsibilities of your job?

A. My duty, according to the Society of Professional Journalists, is to seek the truth and report it accurately. On a daily basis, that means monitoring developments on my beat, cultivating sources, conducting interviews, tracking down documents, writing stories and checking facts.

Working with photographers, page designers, and editors is also a part of my job. Most reporters at the *Monitor* write three to five stories a week. We take turns working on larger projects that involve lots of research or time in the field. Everyone handles briefs and fun little features.

Q. What are some of the issues on which you've focused as a reporter?

A. I've covered city hall, the New Hampshire State House and the 2004 presidential primary and general election. Now I'm one of the few reporters in the nation focusing full time on aging and eldercare.

Q. What is your typical workday like? Do interact with many people, either in person or over the phone/ e-mail?
A. Every day is different. Most of the time, I work from 10 A.M. to 6 P.M., with a deadline around 5:30 P.M. But when news breaks, we have to be ready to go. I've been hauled out of bed before sunrise to cover widespread flooding and left the office well past midnight after filing a story about a nighttime city council meeting. I conduct as many interviews as I can in person, but I use the phone for background information or to reach people who live far away.

Q. What do you find most rewarding about your job?
A. I'm never bored. Being a reporter is like having permission to talk to anyone, ask random questions, and go interesting places.

Q. What are some of the challenges of being a reporter?
A. The hours are long and unpredictable. The pay isn't great, especially when you're just starting out. The work, despite the many people you meet, gets lonely.

Q. What kinds of training and education did you need to become a reporter?
A. I have a bachelor's degree in English from the University of New Hampshire, as well as a minor in business. I've also completed fellowships with the Poynter Institute and the New York Times Foundation.

You should aim for a broad knowledge base in history, economics, civics and literature, but the best way to learn to write for a newspaper is to write for a newspaper. I worked as a staff writer and, later, an editor for UNH's student paper. I gained experience and stockpiled clips for my portfolio.

Q. What would you say are the most important skills and personal qualities for someone in your career?
A. Curiosity about how the world works, respect for people of many backgrounds, and attention to detail.

Q. How have changes in technology transformed the way you do your job?

A. I can't imagine my job without the Internet or my cell phone. I also use a digital voice recorder in the field and we occasionally load sound clips onto our Web site.

Q. What advice would you give someone interested in becoming a reporter?

A. Read. Write. Read some more. Call your local paper and ask if they take interns. Ask the local education reporter if you can follow her around for a day. Write for your school paper. Keep a journal. Watch the news on TV. Question everything.

Science and Medical Writers

OVERVIEW

Science and medical writers translate technical medical and scientific information so it can be disseminated to the general public and professionals in the field. Science and medical writers research, interpret, write, and edit scientific and medical information. Their work often appears in books, technical studies and reports, magazine and trade journal articles, newspapers, company newsletters, and on Web sites, and may be used for radio and television broadcasts.

HISTORY

The skill of writing has existed for thousands of years. Papyrus fragments with writing by ancient Egyptians date from about 3000 B.C., and archaeological findings show that the Chinese had developed books by about 1300 B.C. A number of technical obstacles had to be overcome before printing and the modern writing profession developed.

The modern age of publishing began in the 18th century. Printing became mechanized, and the novel, magazine, and newspaper were developed. Developments in the printing trades, photoengraving, retailing, and the availability of capital produced a boom in newspapers and magazines in the 19th century. Further mechanization in the printing field, such as the use of Linotype machines, high-speed rotary presses, and color-reproduction processes, set the stage for still further growth in the book, newspaper, and magazine industry.

QUICK FACTS

School Subjects
Biology
English
Journalism

Personal Skills
Communication/ideas
Technical/scientific

Work Environment
Primarily indoors
Primarily multiple locations

Minimum Education Level
Bachelor's degree

Salary Range
$24,320 to $46,420 to $89,940+

Certification or Licensing
Voluntary

Outlook
About as fast as the average

DOT
131

GOE
01.02.01

NOC
5121

O*NET-SOC
27-3042.00, 27-3043.01

The History of Popular-Science Magazines

The oldest continuously published magazine in the United States, *Scientific American,* was founded in 1845 by Rufus Porter. Initially intended to explain scientific developments primarily to scientists who were not experts in the reported field, the magazine now explains new research to a lay audience. Other popular-science magazines include *American Scientist, Discover, Science News, Seed,* and *Popular Science,* which was first published in 1872.

The broadcasting industry has also contributed to the development of the professional writer. Film, radio, and television are sources of entertainment, information, and education that provide employment for thousands of writers. Today, the computer industry and the Internet have created the need for more writers.

As our world becomes more complex and people require more information, professional writers have become increasingly important. And, as medicine and science take giant steps forward and discoveries are being made every day that impact our lives, skilled science and medical writers are needed to document these changes and disseminate the information to the general public and to more specialized audiences.

THE JOB

Science and medical writers usually write about subjects related to these fields. Because the medical and scientific subject areas may sometimes overlap, writers often find that they do science writing as well as medical writing. For instance, a medical writer might write about a scientific study that has an impact on the medical field.

Medical and science writing may be targeted for the printed page, the broadcast media, or the Web. It can be specific to one product and one type of writing, such as writing medical information and consumer publications for a specific drug line produced by a pharmaceutical company. Research facilities hire writers to edit reports or write about their scientific or medical studies. Writers who are public information officers write press releases that inform the public about the latest scientific or medical research findings. Educational publishers use writers to write or edit educational materials for the medical profession. Science and medical writers also write online articles or interactive courses that are distributed over the Internet.

According to Barbara Gastel, M.D., coordinator of the master of science program in science and technology journalism at Texas A&M University, many science and technology-related industries are using specialized writers to communicate complex subjects to the public. "In addition," she says, "opportunities exist in the popular media. Newspapers, radio, TV, and the Web have writers who specialize in covering medical and scientific subjects."

Science and medical writers usually write for the general public. They translate high-tech information into articles and reports that the general public and the media can understand. Good writers who cover the subjects thoroughly have inquisitive minds and enjoy looking for additional information that might add to their articles. They research the topic to gain a thorough understanding of their subject matter. This may require hours of research on the Internet, or in corporate, university, or public libraries. Writers always need good background information regarding a subject before they can write about it.

In order to get the information required, writers may interview professionals such as doctors, pharmacists, scientists, engineers, managers, and others who are familiar with the subject. Writers must know how to present the information clearly so it can be easily understood. This requires knowing the audience and how to reach them. For example, an article may need graphs, photos, or historical facts. Writers sometimes enlist the help of technical or medical illustrators or engineers in order to add a visual dimension to their work.

For example, if reporting on a new heart surgery procedure that will soon be available to the public, writers may need to illustrate how that surgery is performed and what areas of the heart are affected. A writer might give a basic overview of how the healthy heart works, show a diseased heart in comparison, and report on how this surgery can help the patient. The public will also want to know how many people are affected by this disease, what the symptoms are, how many procedures have been done successfully, where they were performed, what the recovery time is, and if there are any complications. In addition, interviews with doctors and patients can add a personal touch to the story.

Broadcast media need short, precise articles that can be transmitted in a specific time allotment. Writers usually need to work quickly because news-related stores have tight deadlines. Because science and medicine can be so complex, science and medical writers also need to help the audience understand and evaluate the information. Writing for the Web encompasses most journalistic guidelines including time constraints and sometimes space constraints.

Some science and medical writers specialize in their subject matter. For instance, a medical writer may write only about heart disease and earn a reputation as the best writer in that subject area. Science writers may limit their writing or research to environmental science subjects, or may be even more specific and focus only on air pollution issues.

According to Jeanie Davis, president of the Southeast Chapter of the American Medical Writers Association, "Medical writing can take several different avenues. You may be a consumer medical writer, write technical medical research, or write about health care issues. Some choose to be medical editors and edit reports written by researchers. Sometimes this medical research must be translated into reports and news releases that the public can understand. Today many writers write for the Web." Davis adds, "It is a very dynamic profession, always changing."

Dr. Gastel says, "This career can have various appeals. People can combine their interest in science or medicine with their love of writing. It is a good field for a generalist who likes science and doesn't want to be tied to research in one area. Plus, it is always fun to get things published."

Some writers may choose to be freelance writers either on a full- or part-time basis, or to supplement other jobs. Freelance science and medical writers are self-employed writers who work with small and large companies, health care organizations, research institutions, or publishing firms on a contract or hourly basis. They may specialize in writing about a specific scientific or medical subject for one or two clients, or they may write about a broad range of subjects for a number of different clients. Many freelance writers write articles, papers, or reports, and then attempt to get them published in newspapers, trade, or consumer publications.

REQUIREMENTS

High School

If you are considering a writing career, you should take English, journalism, and communication courses in high school. Computer classes will also be helpful. If you know in high school that you want to do scientific or medical writing, it would be to your advantage to take biology, physiology, chemistry, physics, math, health, psychology, and other science-related courses. If your school offers journalism courses and you have the chance to work on the school newspaper or yearbook, you should take advantage of these opportunities. Part-time employment at health care facilities, newspapers, publishing companies, or scientific research facilities can also provide experience and insight regarding this career. Volunteer opportunities are also available in hospitals and nursing homes.

Postsecondary Training

Although not all writers are college-educated, today's jobs almost always require a bachelor's degree. Many writers earn an undergraduate degree in English, journalism, or liberal arts and then obtain a master's degree in a communications field such as medical or science writing. A good liberal arts education is important since you are often required to write about many subject areas. Science and medical-related courses are highly recommended. You should investigate internship programs that give you experience in the communications department of a corporation, medical institution, or research facility. Some newspapers, magazines, or public relations firms also have internships that give you the opportunity to write.

Some people find that after working as a writer, their interests are strong in the medical or science fields and they evolve into that writing specialty. They may return to school and enter a master's degree program or take some additional courses related specifically to science and medical writing. Similarly, science majors or people in the medical fields may find that they like the writing aspect of their jobs and return to school to pursue a career as a medical or science writer.

Certification or Licensing

Certification is not mandatory; however, certification programs are available from various organizations and institutions. The American Medical Writers Association Education Program offers an extensive continuing education and certification program.

Other Requirements

If you are considering a career as a medical or science writer, you should enjoy writing, be able to write well, and be able to express your ideas and those of others clearly. You should have an excellent knowledge of the English language and have superb grammar and spelling skills. You should be skilled in research techniques and be computer literate and familiar with software programs related to writing and publishing. You should be curious, enjoy learning about new things, and have an interest in science or medicine. You need to be detail-oriented since many of your writing assignments will require that you obtain and relay accurate and detailed information. Interpersonal skills are also important because many jobs require that you interact with and interview professional scientists, engineers, researchers, and medical personnel. You must be able to meet deadlines and work under pressure.

EXPLORING

As a high school or college student, you can test your interest and aptitude in the field of writing by serving as a reporter or writer on school newspapers, yearbooks, and literary magazines. Attending writing workshops and taking writing classes will give you the opportunity to practice and sharpen your skills.

Community newspapers and local radio stations often welcome contributions from outside sources, although they may not have the resources to pay for them. Jobs in bookstores, magazine shops, libraries, and even newsstands offer a chance to become familiar with various publications. If you are interested in science writing, try to get a part-time job in a research laboratory, interview science writers, and read good science writing in major newspapers such as the *New York Times* or the *Wall Street Journal*. Similarly, if your interest is medical writing, work or volunteer in a health care facility, visit with people who do medical writing, and read medical articles in those newspapers previously listed. You may also find it helpful to read publications such as the *American Medical Writers Association Journal*. For more information visit http://www. amwa.org.

Information on writing as a career may also be obtained by visiting local newspapers, publishing houses, or radio and television stations and interviewing some of the writers who work there. Career conferences and other guidance programs frequently include speakers from local or national organizations who can provide information on communication careers.

Some professional organizations such as the Society for Technical Communication welcome students as members and have special student membership rates and career information. In addition, participation in professional organizations gives you the opportunity to meet and visit with people in this career field.

EMPLOYERS

Pharmaceutical and drug companies, medical research institutions, government organizations, insurance companies, health care facilities, nonprofit organizations, medical publishers, medical associations, and other medical-related industries employ medical writers.

Science writers may also be employed by medical-related industries. In addition, they are employed by scientific research companies, government research facilities, federal, state, and local agencies, manufacturing companies, research and development departments of corporations, and the chemical industries. Large universities and hospitals often employ science writers. Large technology-based corporations and industrial research groups also hire science writers.

Many science and medical writers are employed, often on a freelance basis, by newspapers, magazines, and the broadcast industries as well. Internet publishing is a growing field that hires science and medical writers. Corporations that deal with the medical or science industries also hire specialty writers as their public information officers or to lead communications departments within their facilities.

STARTING OUT

A fair amount of experience is required to gain a high-level position in this field. Most writers start out in entry-level positions. These jobs may be listed with college placement offices, or you may apply directly to the employment departments of corporations, institutions, universities, research facilities, nonprofit organizations, and government facilities that hire science and medical writers. Many firms now hire writers directly upon application or recommendation of college professors and placement offices. Want ads in newspapers and trade journals are another source for jobs. Serving an internship in college can give you the advantage of knowing people who can give you personal recommendations.

Internships are also excellent ways to build your portfolio. Employers in the communications field are usually interested in seeing samples of your published writing assembled in an organized portfolio or scrapbook. Working on your college's magazine or newspaper staff can help you build a portfolio. Sometimes small, regional magazines will also buy articles or assign short pieces for you to write. You should attempt to build your portfolio with good writing samples. Be sure to include the type of writing you are interested in doing, if possible.

You may need to begin your career as a junior writer or editor and work your way up. This usually involves library research, preparation of rough drafts for part or all of a report, cataloging, and other related writing tasks. These are generally carried on under the supervision of a senior writer.

Many science and medical writers enter the field after working in public relations departments, the medical profession, or science-related industries. They may use their skills to transfer to specialized writing positions or they may take additional courses or graduate work that focuses on writing or documentation skills.

ADVANCEMENT

Writers with only an undergraduate degree may choose to get a graduate degree in science or medical writing, corporate communications, document design, or a related program. An advanced degree may open doors to more career options.

Many experienced science and medical writers are often promoted to head writing, documentation, or public relations departments within corporations or institutions. Some may become recognized experts in their field and their writings may be in demand by trade journals, newspapers, magazines, and the broadcast industry.

As freelance writers prove themselves and work successfully with clients, they may be able to demand increased contract fees or hourly rates.

EARNINGS

Although there are no specific salary studies for science and medical writers, salary information for all writers is available. The U.S. Department of Labor reports that the median annual salary for writers in 2005 was $46,420. Salaries ranged from less than $24,320 to more than $89,940. Median annual earnings for technical writers were $55,160 in 2005. The lowest-paid 10 percent earned less than $33,250, while the highest-paid 10 percent earned more than $87,550.

According to the Society for Technical Communication, the median salary for entry-level technical writers was $42,500 in 2004. Mid-level writers earned $51,500, and senior-level writers in non-supervisory positions earned $66,000.

Freelance writers' earnings can vary depending on their expertise, reputation, and the articles they are contracted to write.

Most full-time writing positions offer benefits such as insurance, sick leave, and paid vacation. Some jobs also provide tuition reimbursement and retirement benefits. Freelance writers must pay for their own insurance. However, there are professional associations that may offer group insurance rates for its members.

WORK ENVIRONMENT

The work environment for science and medical writers depends on the type of writing and the employer. Generally, writers work in an office or research environment. Writers for the news media sometimes work in noisy surroundings. Some writers travel to research information and conduct interviews while other employers may confine research to local libraries or the Internet. In addition, some employers require writers to conduct research interviews over the phone, rather than in person.

Although the workweek usually runs 35 to 40 hours in a normal office setting, many writers may have to work overtime to cover a story, interview people, meet deadlines, or to disseminate information in a timely manner. The newspaper and broadcasting industries deliver the news 24 hours a day, seven days a week. Writers often work nights and weekends to meet press deadlines or to cover a late-developing story.

Each day may bring new and interesting situations. Some stories may even take writers to exotic locations with a chance to interview famous people and write about timely topics. Other assignments may be boring or they may take place in less than desirable settings, where interview subjects may be rude and unwilling to talk. One of the most difficult elements for writers may be meeting deadlines or gathering information. People who are the most content as writers work well with deadline pressure.

OUTLOOK

According to the U.S. Department of Labor, there is a lot of competition for writing and editing jobs, and growth in writing careers should occur at an average rate through 2014. Opportunities should be very good for science and medical writers, as continued developments in these fields will drive the need for skilled writers to put complex information in terms that a wide and varied audience can understand.

FOR MORE INFORMATION

For information on careers as science and medical writers, contact the following organizations:
American Medical Writers Association
40 West Gude Drive, Suite 101
Rockville, MD 20850-1192
Tel: 301-294-5303

Email: amwa@amwa.org
http://www.amwa.org

National Association of Science Writers Inc.
PO Box 890
Hedgesville, WV 25427-0890
Tel: 304-754-5077
http://www.nasw.org

For information on scholarships and student memberships aimed at those preparing for a career in technical communication, contact
Society for Technical Communication
901 North Stuart Street, Suite 904
Arlington, VA 22203-1822
Tel: 703-522-4114
Email: stc@src.org
http://www.stc.org

Screenwriters

OVERVIEW

Screenwriters write scripts for entertainment, education, training, sales, television, and films. Screenwriters may choose themes themselves, or they may write on a theme assigned by a producer or director, sometimes adapting plays or novels into screenplays. Screenwriting is an art, a craft, and a business. It is a career that requires imagination and creativity, the ability to tell a story using both dialogue and pictures, and the ability to negotiate with producers and studio executives.

HISTORY

In 1894, Thomas Edison invented the kinetograph to take a series of pictures of actions staged specifically for the camera. In October of the same year, the first film opened at Hoyt's Theatre in New York. It consisted of a series of acts performed by such characters as a strongman, a contortionist, and trained animals. Even in these earliest motion pictures, the plot or sequence of actions the film would portray was written down before filming began.

Newspaperman Roy McCardell was the first person to be hired for the specific job of writing for motion pictures. He wrote captions for photographs in a weekly entertainment publication. When he was employed by Biograph to write 10 scenarios, or stories, at $10 apiece, it caused a flood of newspapermen to try their hand at screenwriting.

The early films ran only about a minute and typically captured scenes of movement and exotic places. These films eventually grew into narrative films running between nine and 15 minutes. The demand for original plots led to the development of story departments at each of the motion picture companies in the period from 1910 to 1915. The story departments were responsible for writing the stories and also for reading and evaluating material that came from outside sources. Stories usually came from writers, but some were purchased from actors on the lot. The actor Genevieve (Gene) Gauntier was paid $20 per reel of film for her first scenarios.

There was a continuing need for scripts because usually a studio bought a story one month, filmed the next, and released the film the month after. Some of the most popular stories in these early films were westerns and comedies.

Longer story films began to use titles, and as motion pictures became longer and more sophisticated, so did the titles. In 1909–10, there was an average of 80 feet of title per 1,000 feet of film. By 1926, the average increased to 250 feet of title per 1,000 feet. The titles included dialogue, description, and historical background.

In 1920, the first Screen Writers Guild was established to ensure fair treatment of writers, and in 1927, the Academy of Motion Picture Arts and Sciences was formed, including a branch for writers. The first sound film, *The Jazz Singer*, was also produced in 1927. Screenwriting changed dramatically to adapt to the new technology.

From the 1950s to the 1980s, the studios gradually declined, and more independent film companies and individuals were able to break into the motion picture industry. The television industry began to thrive in the 1950s, further increasing the number of opportunities for screenwriters. During the 1960s, people began to graduate from the first education programs developed specifically for screenwriting.

Today, most Americans have spent countless hours viewing programs on television and movie screens. Familiarity with these mediums has led many writers to attempt writing screenplays. This has created an intensely fierce marketplace with many more screenplays being rejected than accepted each year.

THE JOB

Screenwriters write dramas, comedies, soap operas, adventures, westerns, documentaries, newscasts, and training films. They may write original stories, or get inspiration from newspapers, magazines, books, or other sources. They may also write scripts for continuing television series. *Continuity writers* in broadcasting create station announcements, previews of coming shows, and advertising copy for local sponsors. Broadcasting scriptwriters usually work in a team, writing for a certain audience, to fill a certain time slot.

Motion picture writers submit an original screenplay or adaptation of a book to a motion picture producer or studio. *Playwrights* submit their plays to drama companies for performance or try to get their work published in book form.

Screenwriters may work on a staff of writers and producers for a large company. Or they may work independently for smaller companies that hire only freelance production teams. Advertising agencies also hire writers, sometimes as staff, sometimes as freelancers.

Scripts are written in a two-column format, one column for dialogue and sound, the other for video instructions. One page of script generally equals about one minute of running time, though it varies. Each page has about 150 words and takes about 20 seconds to read. Screenwriters send a query letter outlining their idea before they submit a script to a production company. Then they send a standard release form and wait at least a month for a response. Studios buy many more scripts than are actually produced, and studios often will buy a script only with provisions that the original writer or another writer will rewrite it to their specifications.

REQUIREMENTS

High School

You can develop your writing skills in English, theater, speech, and journalism classes. Belonging to a debate team can also help you learn how to express your ideas within a specific time allotment and framework. History, government, and foreign language can contribute to a well-rounded education, necessary for creating intelligent scripts. A business course can be useful in understanding the basic business principles of the film industry.

Postsecondary Training

There are no set educational requirements for screenwriters. A college degree is desirable, especially a liberal arts education, which exposes you to a wide range of subjects. An undergraduate or graduate film program will likely include courses in screenwriting, film theory, and other subjects that will teach you about the film industry and its history. A creative writing program will involve you with workshops and seminars that will help you develop fiction-writing skills.

Other Requirements

As a screenwriter, you must be able to create believable characters and develop a story. You must have technical skills, such as dialogue writing, creating plots, and doing research. In addition to creativity and originality, you also need an understanding of the marketplace for your work. You should be aware of what kinds of scripts are in demand by producers. Word processing skills are also helpful.

EXPLORING

One of the best ways to learn about screenwriting is to read and study scripts. It is advisable to watch a motion picture while simultaneously following the script. The scripts for such classic films as *Casablanca*, *Network*, and *Chinatown* are often taught in college screenwriting courses. You should read film-industry publications, such as *Daily Variety* (http://www.variety.com), *Hollywood Reporter* (http://www.hollywoodreporter.com), and *The Hollywood Scriptwriter* (http://www.hollywoodscriptwriter.com). There are a number of books about screenwriting, but they are often written by those outside of the industry. These books are best used primarily for learning about the format required for writing a screenplay. There are also computer software programs that assist with screenplay formatting.

The Sundance Institute, a Utah-based production company, accepts unsolicited scripts from those who have read the Institute's submission guidelines. Every January they choose a few scripts and invite the writers to a five-day program of one-on-one sessions with professionals. The process is repeated in June and also includes a videotaping of sections of chosen scripts. The Institute doesn't produce features, but they can often introduce writers to those who do. (For contact information, see the end of this article.)

Most states offer grants for emerging and established screenwriters and other artists. Contact your state's art council for guidelines and application materials. In addition, several arts groups and associations hold annual contests for screenwriters. To find out more about screenwriting contests, consult a reference work such as *The Writer's Market* (http://www.writersmarket.com).

Students may try to get their work performed locally. A teacher may be able to help you submit your work to a local radio or television station or to a publisher of plays.

EMPLOYERS

Most screenwriters work on a freelance basis, contracting with production companies for individual projects. Those who work for television may contract with a TV production company for a certain number of episodes or seasons.

Women in Screenwriting

Women screenwriters were much more prominent in the industry in the early days of filmmaking; half of the films made before 1925 were written by women, such as Frances Marion (*Stella Dallas, The Scarlet Letter*) and Anita Loos (*The Women*). Marion was the highest-paid screenwriter from 1916 to the 1930s, and she served as the first vice president of the Writer's Guild. Though a smaller percentage of feature films written by women are produced today, more women screenwriters have won Academy Awards since 1985 than in all previous years. Among recent Oscar winners are Ruth Prawer Jhabvala (*Howard's End*) and Sofia Coppola (*Lost in Translation*).

STARTING OUT

The first step to getting a screenplay produced is to write a letter to the script editor of a production company describing yourself, your training, and your work. Ask if the editors would be interested in reading one of your scripts. You should also pursue a manager or agent by sending a brief letter describing your project. A list of agents is available from the Writers Guild of America (WGA). If you receive an invitation to submit more, you'll then prepare a synopsis or treatment of the screenplay, which is usually from one to 10 pages. It should be in the form of a narrative short story, with little or no dialogue.

Whether you are a beginning or experienced screenwriter, it is best to have an agent, since studios, producers, and stars often return unsolicited manuscripts unopened to protect themselves from plagiarism charges. Agents provide access to studios and producers, interpret contracts, and negotiate deals.

It is wise to register your script (online registration is $10 for members and $20 for nonmembers) with the WGA. Although registration offers no legal protection, it is proof that on a specific date you came up with a particular idea, treatment, or script. You should also keep a detailed journal that lists the contacts you've made, including the people who have read your script.

ADVANCEMENT

Competition is stiff among screenwriters, and a beginner will find it difficult to break into the field. More opportunities become available as a screenwriter gains experience and a reputation, but that is a process that can take many years. Rejection is a common occurrence in the field of screenwriting. Most successful screenwriters have had to send their screenplays to numerous production companies before they find one who likes their work.

Once they have sold some scripts, screenwriters may be able to join the WGA. Membership with the WGA guarantees the screenwriter a minimum wage for a production and other benefits such as arbitration. Some screenwriters, however, writing for minor productions, can have regular work and successful careers without WGA membership.

Those screenwriters who manage to break into the business can benefit greatly from recognition in the industry. In addition to creating their own scripts, some writers are also hired to "doctor" the scripts of others, using their expertise to revise scripts for production. If a film proves very successful, a screenwriter will be able to command higher payment, and will be able to work on high-profile productions. Some of the most talented screenwriters receive awards from the industry, most notably the Academy Award for best original or adapted screenplay.

EARNINGS

Wages for screenwriters are nearly impossible to track. Some screenwriters make hundreds of thousands of dollars from their scripts, while others write and film their own scripts without any payment at all, relying on backers and loans. Screenwriter Joe Eszter made entertainment news in the early 1990s when he received $3 million for each of his treatments for *Basic Instinct*, *Jade*, and *Showgirls*. In the early 2000s, a number of scripts by first-time screenwriters were sold for between $500,000 and $1 million. Typically, a writer will earn a percentage (approximately 1 percent) of the film's budget. Obviously, a lower budget film pays considerably less than a big production, starting at $15,000 or less. According to the WGA, the median income for WGA members was $87,104 in 2001. Earnings ranged from less than $28,091 to more than $567,726. Screenwriters who are WGA members also are eligible to receive health benefits.

WORK ENVIRONMENT

Screenwriters who choose to freelance have the freedom to write when and where they choose. They must be persistent and patient; only one in 20 to 30 purchased or optioned screenplays is actually produced.

Screenwriters who work on the staff of a large company, for a television series, or under contract to a motion picture company may share writing duties with others.

Screenwriters who do not live in Hollywood or New York City will likely have to travel to attend script conferences. They may even have to relocate for several weeks while a project is in production. Busy periods before and during film production are followed by long periods of inactivity and solitude. This forces many screenwriters, especially those just getting started in the field, to work other jobs and pursue other careers while they develop their talent and craft.

OUTLOOK

There is intense competition in the television and motion picture industries. There are currently 11,000 members of the WGA. A 2001 report by the WGA found that only about 50 percent of its members were actually employed the previous year. The report also focused on the opportunities for women and minority screenwriters. Despite employment for minority screenwriters substantially increasing, employment for women changed little in that decade. Eighty percent of those writing for feature films are white males. Though this domination in the industry will eventually change because of efforts by women and minority filmmakers, the change may be slow in coming. The success of independent cinema, which has introduced a number of women and minority filmmakers to the industry, will continue to contribute to this change.

As cable television expands and digital technology allows for more programming, new opportunities will emerge. Television networks continue to need new material and new episodes for long-running series. Studios are always looking for new angles on action, adventure, horror, and comedy, and especially romantic comedy stories. The demand for new screenplays should increase slightly in the next decade, but the number of screenwriters is growing at a faster rate. Writers will continue to find opportunities in advertising agencies and educational and training video production houses.

FOR MORE INFORMATION

For guidelines on submitting a script for consideration for the Sundance Institute's screenwriting program, send a self-addressed stamped envelope to the Institute or visit the following Web site:

Sundance Institute
8530 Wilshire Boulevard, 3rd Floor
Beverly Hills, CA, 90211-3114
Tel: 310-360-1981
Email: la@sundance.org
http://www.sundance.org

To learn more about the film industry, to read interviews and articles by noted screenwriters, and to find links to many other screenwriting-related sites on the Internet, visit the Web sites of the WGA.
Writers Guild of America (WGA)
East Chapter
555 West 57th Street, Suite 1230
New York, NY 10019-2925
Tel: 212-767-7800
http://www.wgaeast.org

Writers Guild of America (WGA)
West Chapter
7000 West Third Street
Los Angeles, CA 90048-4321
Tel: 800-548-4532
http://www.wga.org

Visit the following Web site to read useful articles on screenwriting:
Screenwriters Utopia
http://www.screenwritersutopia.com

Songwriters

OVERVIEW

Songwriters write the words and music for songs, including songs for recordings, advertising jingles, and theatrical performances. We hear the work of songwriters every day, and yet most songwriters remain anonymous, even if a song's performer is famous. Many songwriters perform their own songs.

HISTORY

Songwriting played an important part in the growth of the United States. The early pioneers wrote songs as a way to socialize and relax. Some of the difficult experiences of traveling, competing for land, farming, and hunting for food were put into words by early songwriters, and the words set to music, for the guitar, banjo, piano, and other instruments. Francis Scott Key became famous for writing the words to the "Star Spangled Banner," set to a popular drinking tune.

Toward the end of the 19th century, sheet music was sold by hundreds of publishing companies, centered in New York City in what became known as Tin Pan Alley. This name was coined by a songwriter and journalist named Monroe Rosenfeld. The name referred to the sounds of many voices and pianos coming from the open windows on the street where many of the music publishers were located. By the 1880s, sheet music was sold in the millions; most songs were introduced on the stages of musical theater, vaudeville, and burlesque shows. Radio became an important medium for introducing new songs in the 1920s, followed by the introduction of sound movies in the 1930s. Sheet music became less important as musical recordings were introduced. This presented difficulties for the songwriter and

QUICK FACTS

School Subjects
English
Music

Personal Skills
Artistic
Communication/ideas

Work Environment
Primarily indoors
Primarily one location

Minimum Education Level
High school diploma

Salary Range
$20,000 to $50,000 to
$100,000+

Certification or Licensing
None available

Outlook
About as fast as the average

DOT
131

GOE
01.05.02

NOC
5132

O*NET-SOC
27-2041.02, 27-2041.03

A songwriter composes a new song. *(Photodisc)*

publisher, because the sales of sheet music were easier to control. In the 1940s, the first associations for protecting the rights of the song-writers and publishers were formed; among the benefits songwriters received were royalties for each time a song they had written was recorded, performed, or played on the radio or in film.

By the 1950s, Tin Pan Alley no longer referred to a specific area in New York but was a term used nationwide to denote popular songs in general, and especially a type of simple melody and sentimental and often silly lyrics that dominated the pop music industry. The rise of rock and roll music in the 1950s put an end to Tin Pan Alley's dominance. Many performers began to write their own songs, a trend that became particularly important in the 1960s. In the late 1970s, a new type of songwriting emerged. Rap music, featuring words chanted over a musical background, in some ways seemed to bring songwriting full circle, back to the oral traditions of its origins.

THE JOB

There are many different ways to write a song. A song may begin with a few words (the lyrics) or with a few notes of a melody, or a song may be suggested by an idea, theme, or product. A song may come about in a flash of inspiration or may be developed slowly over a long period of time. Songwriters may work alone, or as part of a team, in which one person concentrates on the lyrics while another person concentrates on the music. Sometimes there may be several people working on the same song.

"One of the most important things," says songwriter Beth McBride, "is collecting your ideas, even if they're only fragments of ideas, and writing them down. Sometimes a song comes to me from beginning to end, but I can't always rely on inspiration. A lot of my writing has been personal, derived from experience and also from the observation of others' experiences." McBride performed for a decade with the band B and the Hot Notes, for which she wrote and recorded original music. After she left the band, she focused on writing and performing her own songs, and released her first CD, *Recovering Grace*, in 2000.

Most popular songs require words, or lyrics, and some songwriters may concentrate on writing the words to a song. These songwriters are called *lyricists*. Events, experiences, or emotions may inspire a lyricist to write lyrics. A lyricist may also be contracted to write the words for a jingle or musical, or to adapt the words from an existing song for another project.

Some songwriters do no more than write the words to a potential song, and leave it to others to develop a melody and musical accompaniment for the words. They may sell the words to a music publisher, or work in a team to create a finished song from the lyric. Some lyricists specialize in writing the words for advertising jingles. They are usually employed by advertising agencies and may work on several different products at once, often under pressure of a deadline.

In songwriting teams, one member may be a lyricist, while the other member is a *composer*. The development of a song can be a highly collaborative process. The composer might suggest topics for the song to the lyricist; the lyricist might suggest a melody to the composer. Other times, the composer plays a musical piece for the lyricist, and the lyricist tries to create lyrics to fit with that piece.

Composers of popular music generally have a strong musical background, and often perform music as well. They must have an understanding of many musical styles, so that they can develop the music that will fit a project's needs. Composers work with a variety of musical and electronic equipment, including computers, to produce and record their music. They develop the different parts for the different musical instruments needed to play the song. They also work with musicians who will play and record the song, and the composer conducts or otherwise directs the musicians as the song is played.

Songwriters, composers, and musicians often make use of MIDI (musical instrument digital interface) technology to produce sounds through synthesizers, drum machines, and samplers. These sounds are usually controlled by a computer, and the composer or songwriter can mix, alter, and refine the sounds using mixing boards and computer software. Like analog or acoustic instruments, which produce sounds as a string or reed or drum head vibrates with air, MIDI creates digital "vibrations" that can produce sounds similar to acoustic instruments or highly unusual sounds invented by the songwriter. Synthesizers and other sound-producing machines may each have their own keyboard or playing mechanism, or be linked through one or more keyboards. They may also be controlled through the computer, or with other types of controls, such as a guitar controller, which plays like a guitar, or foot controls. Songs can be stored in the computer, or transferred to tape or compact disc.

Many, if not most, songwriters combine both the work of a lyricist and the work of a composer. Often, a songwriter will perform his or her own songs as well, whether as a singer, a member of a band, or both. Playing guitar has helped McBride in the writing of lyrics and music. "My songwriting has become more sophisticated as my playing has become more sophisticated," she says.

For most songwriters, writing a song is only the first part of their job. After a song is written, songwriters usually produce a "demo" of the song, so that the client or potential purchaser of the song can hear how it sounds. Songwriters contract with recording studios, studio musicians, and recording engineers to produce a version of the song. The songwriter then submits the song to a publishing house, record company, recording artist, film studio, or others, who will then decide if the song is appropriate for their needs. Often, a songwriter will produce several versions of a song, or submit several different songs for a particular project. There is always a chance that one, some, or all of their songs will be rejected.

REQUIREMENTS

High School

You should take courses in music that involve singing, playing instruments, and studying the history of music. Theater and speech classes will help you to understand the nature of performing, and involve you in writing dramatic pieces. You should study poetry in an English class, and try your hand at composing poetry in different forms. Language skills can also be honed in foreign-language classes and by working on student literary magazines. An understanding of how people act and think can influence you as a lyricist, so take courses in psychology and sociology.

Postsecondary Training
There are no real requirements for entering the field of songwriting. All songwriters, however, will benefit from musical training, including musical theory and musical notation. Learning to play one or more instruments, such as the piano or guitar, will be especially helpful in writing songs. Not all songwriters need to be able to sing, but it can be helpful.

Songwriting is an extremely competitive field. Despite a lack of formal educational requirements, prospective songwriters are encouraged to continue their education through high school and preferably toward a college degree. Much of the musical training a songwriter needs, however, can also be learned informally. In general, you should have a background in music theory, and in arrangement and orchestration for multiple instruments. You should be able to read music, and be able to write it in the proper musical notation. You should have a good sense of the sounds each type of musical instrument produces, alone and in combination. Understanding harmony is important, as is a proficiency in or understanding of a variety of styles of music. Studies in music history will also help develop this understanding.

On the technical side, you should understand the various features, capabilities, and requirements of modern recording techniques. You should be familiar with MIDI and computer technology, as these play important roles in composing, playing, and recording music today.

There are several organizations that help lyricists, songwriters, and composers. The Songwriters Guild of America (http://www.songwritersguild.com) offers weekly song evaluation workshops in select cities. The Nashville Songwriters Association (http://www.nashvillesongwriters.com) offers workshops, seminars, and other services, as well as giving annual awards to songwriters. The Songwriters and Lyricists Club (PO Box 023304, Brooklyn, NY 11202-0066) provides contacts for songwriters with music-business professionals. These, and other organizations, offer songwriting workshops and other training seminars.

Other Requirements
Many elements of songwriting cannot really be learned but are a matter of inborn talent. A creative imagination and the ability to

invent melodies and combine melodies into a song are essential parts of a songwriting career. As you become more familiar with your own talents, and with the songwriting process, you'll learn to develop and enhance your creative skills.

"I enjoy observing," Beth McBride says. "I also enjoy the challenge of finding the most succinct way of saying something and making it poetic. I enjoy the process of finding that perfect turn of phrase. I really love language and words."

EXPLORING

The simplest way to gain experience in songwriting is to learn to play a musical instrument, especially the piano or guitar, and to invent your own songs. Joining a rock group is a way to gain experience writing music for several musicians. Most schools and communities have orchestras, bands, and choruses that are open to performers. Working on a student-written musical show is ideal training if you want to be a songwriter.

If you have your own computer, consider investing in software, a keyboard, and other devices that will allow you to experiment with sounds, recording, and writing and composing your own songs. While much of this equipment is expensive, there are plenty of affordable keyboards, drum machines, and software programs available today. Your school's music department may also have such equipment available.

EMPLOYERS

Most songwriters work freelance, competing for contracts to write songs for a particular artist, television show, video program, or for contracts with musical publishers and advertising agencies. They meet with clients to determine the nature of the project and to get an idea of what kind of music the client seeks, the budget for the project, the time in which the project is expected to be completed, and in what form the work is to be submitted. Many songwriters work under contract with one or more music publishing houses. Usually, they must fulfill a certain quota of new songs each year. These songwriters receive a salary, called an advance or draw, that is often paid by the week. Once a song has been published, the money earned by the song goes to pay back the songwriter's draw. A percentage of the money earned by the song over and above the amount of the draw goes to the songwriter as a royalty. Other songwriters are employed by so-called *jingle houses*, companies that supply music for advertising commercials. Whereas most songwriters work in their own homes or offices, these songwriters work at the jingle house's offices. Film, television, and video production studios may also employ songwriters on their staff.

STARTING OUT

Songwriting is a very competitive career and difficult to break into for a beginner. The number of high-paying projects is limited. Beginning songwriters often start their careers writing music for themselves or as part of a musical group. They may also offer their services to student films, student and local theater productions, church groups, and other religious and nonprofit organizations, often for free or for a low fee.

Many songwriters get their start while performing their own music in clubs and other venues; they may be approached by a music publisher, who contracts them for a number of songs. Other song-

Learn More about It

Blume, Jason. *Six Steps to Songwriting Success: Comprehensive Guide to Writing and Marketing Hit Songs*. New York: Watson-Guptill Publications, 1999.

Braheny, John. *The Craft and Business of Songwriting*. 2d ed. Cincinnati, Ohio: F&W Publications, Writers Digest Books, 2001.

Davis, Sheila. *The Songwriter's Idea Book: 40 Strategies to Excite Your Imagination, Help You Design Distinctive Songs, and Keep Your Creative Flow*. Cincinnati, Ohio: F&W Publications, Writers Digest Books, 1995.

Leikin, Molly-Ann. *How to Make a Good Song a Hit Song: Rewriting and Marketing Your Lyrics and Music*. Milwaukee, Wisc.: Hal Leonard Publishing, 1995.

Mitchell, Kevin M. *Essential Songwriters Rhyming Dictionary*. Van Nuys, Calif.: Alfred Publishing Company, 1996.

Perricone, Jack. *Melody in Songwriting: Tools and Techniques for Writing Hit Songs*. New York: Hal Leonard Publishing, 2000.

Scott, Richard J. *Money Chords: A Songwriter's Sourcebook of Popular Chord Progressions*. New York: Writers Club Press, 2000.

Tucker, Susan. *The Secrets of Songwriting: Leading Songwriters Reveal How to Find Inspiration and Success*. New York; All-worth Press, 2003.

Webb, Jimmy. *Tunesmith: Inside the Art of Songwriting*. New York: Hyperion, 1999.

Zollo, Paul. *Songwriters on Songwriting*. 4th Ed. Cambridge, Mass.: Da Capo Press, 2003.

writers record demos of their songs and try to interest record companies and music publishers. Some songwriters organize showcase performances, renting a local club or hall and inviting music industry people to hear their work. Songwriters may have to approach many companies and publishers before they find one willing to buy their songs. A great deal of making a success in songwriting is in developing contacts with people active in the music industry.

Some songwriters get their start in one of the few entry-level positions available. Songwriters aspiring to become composers for film and television can find work as orchestrators or copyists in film houses. Other songwriters may find work for music agents and publishers, which will give them an understanding of the industry and increase their contacts in the business, as they develop their songwriting skills. Those interested in specializing in advertising jingles may find entry-level work as music production assistants with a jingle house. At first, such jobs may involve making coffee, doing paperwork, and completing other clerical tasks. As you gain more exposure to the process of creating music, you may begin in basic areas of music production, or assist experienced songwriters.

ADVANCEMENT

It is important for a songwriter to develop a strong portfolio of work and a reputation for professionalism. Songwriters who establish a reputation for producing quality work will receive larger and higher-paying projects as their careers progress. They may be contracted to score major motion pictures, or to write songs for major recording artists. Ultimately, they may be able to support themselves on their songwriting alone and also have the ability to choose the projects they will work on.

In order to continue to grow with the music industry, songwriters must be tuned into new musical styles and trends. They must also keep up with developments in music technology. A great deal of time is spent making and maintaining contacts with others in the music industry.

Songwriters specializing in jingles and other commercial products may eventually start up their own jingle house. Other songwriters, especially those who have written a number of hit songs, may themselves become recording artists.

For many songwriters, however, success and advancement is a very personal process. A confidence in your own talent will help you to create better work. "I'm not as vulnerable about my work," Beth McBride says. "And I want to open up my subject matter, to expand and experiment more."

EARNINGS

Songwriters' earnings vary widely, from next to nothing to many millions of dollars. A beginning songwriter may work for free, or for low pay, just to gain experience. A songwriter may sell a jingle to an advertising agency for $1,000 or may receive many thousands of dollars if his or her work is well-known. Royalties from a song may reach $20,000 per year or more per song, and a successful songwriter may earn $100,000 or more per year from the royalties of several songs. A songwriter's earnings may come from a combination of royalties earned on songs and fees from commercial projects.

Those starting as assistants in music production companies or jingle houses may earn as little as $20,000 per year. Experienced songwriters at these companies may earn $50,000 per year or more.

Because most songwriters are freelance, they will have to provide their own health insurance, life insurance, and pension plans. They are usually paid per project, and therefore receive no overtime pay. When facing a deadline, they may have to work more than eight hours a day or 40 hours a week. Also, songwriters are generally responsible for recording their own demos and must pay for recording studio time, studio musicians, and production expenses.

WORK ENVIRONMENT

Songwriters generally possess a strong love for music and, regardless of the level of their success, usually find fulfillment in their careers because they are doing what they love to do. As freelancers, they will control how they spend their day. Freelancers work out of their own home or office, and must have their own instruments, and possibly their own recording equipment as well. Songwriters may also work in recording studios, where conditions can range from noisy and busy to relaxed and quiet.

Writing music can be stressful. When facing a deadline, songwriters may experience a great deal of pressure while trying to get their music just right and on time. They may face a great deal of rejection before they find someone willing to publish or record their songs. Rejection remains a part of the songwriter's life, even after success.

Many songwriters work many years with limited or no success. On the other hand, songwriters experience the joys of creativity, which has its own rewards.

OUTLOOK

Most songwriters are unable to support themselves from their song-writing alone and must hold other part-time or full-time jobs while writing songs in their spare time. The music industry is very competitive, and there are many more songwriters than paying projects. This situation is expected to continue into the next decade.

There are a few bright spots for songwriters. The recent rise of independent filmmaking has created more venues for songwriters to compose film scores. Cable television also provides more opportunities for songwriting, both in the increased number of advertisements and in the growing trend for cable networks to develop their own original programs. Many computer games and software feature songs and music, and this area should grow rapidly in the next decade. Another booming area is the World Wide Web. As more and more companies, organizations, and individuals set up multimedia Web sites, there will be an increased demand for songwriters to create songs and music for these sites. Songwriters with MIDI capability will be in the strongest position to benefit from the growth created by computer uses of music. In another field, legalized gambling has spread to many states in the country, a large number of resorts and theme parks have opened, and as these venues often produce their own musical theater and shows, they will require more songwriters.

The number of hit songs is very small compared to the number of songwriters trying to write them. Success in songwriting therefore requires a combination of hard work, industry connections, and good luck.

FOR MORE INFORMATION

For membership information, contact
American Society of Composers, Authors and Publishers
One Lincoln Plaza
New York, NY 10023-7129
Tel: 212-621-6000
Email: info@ascap.com
http://www.ascap.com

Visit the Songwriter's section of the BMI Web site to learn more about performing rights, music publishing, copyright, and the business of songwriting.
Broadcast Music Inc. (BMI)
320 West 57th Street
New York, NY 10019-3790

Tel: 212-586-2000
http://www.bmi.com

To learn about the annual young composer's competition and other contests, contact
National Association of Composers, USA
PO Box 49256, Barrington Station
Los Angeles, CA 90049-0256
Tel: 818-274-6048
Email: nacusa@music-usa.org
http://www.music-usa.org/nacusa

The SGA offers song critiques and other workshops in select cities. Visit its Web site for further information on such events.
Songwriters Guild of America (SGA)
209 10th Avenue South, Suite 321
Nashville, TN 37203-0743
Tel: 615-742-9945
http://www.songwritersguild.com

Technical Writers and Editors

QUICK FACTS

School Subjects
Business
English

Personal Skills
Communication/ideas
Technical/scientific

Work Environment
Primarily indoors
Primarily one location

Minimum Education Level
Bachelor's degree

Salary Range
$33,250 to $55,160 to
$87,550+

Certification or Licensing
None available

Outlook
About as fast as the average

DOT
131 (writers), 132 (editors)

GOE
01.02.01

NOC
5121; 5122

O*NET-SOC
27-3041.00, 27-3042.00,
27-3043.00

OVERVIEW

Technical writers, sometimes called *technical communicators*, express technical and scientific ideas in easy-to-understand language. *Technical editors* revise written text to correct any errors and make it read smoothly and clearly. They also may coordinate the activities of technical writers, technical illustrators, and other staff in preparing material for publication and oversee the document development and production processes. Technical writers hold about 50,000 jobs in the United States.

HISTORY

Humans have used writing to communicate information for over 5,500 years. Technical writing, though, did not emerge as a specific profession in the United States until the early years of the 20th century. Before that time, engineers, scientists, and researchers did any necessary writing themselves.

During the early 1900s, technology expanded rapidly. The use of machines to manufacture and mass-produce a wide number of products paved the way for more complex and technical products. Scientists and researchers were discovering new technologies and applications for technology, particularly in electronics, medicine, and engineering. The need to record studies and research, and report them to others, grew. Also, as products became more complex, it was necessary to provide information that documented their components, showed how they were assembled, and explained how to install, use, and repair them. By the mid-1920s, writers were being used to help engineers and scientists document their work and prepare technical information for nontechnical audiences.

Editors have work with printers and authors to refine writing and ensure its correctness. They check copies of a printed document to correct any errors made during printing, to rewrite unclear passages, and to correct errors in spelling, grammar, and punctuation. As the need for technical writers grew, so too did the need for technical editors. Editors became more involved in documents before the printing stage, and today work closely with writers as they prepare their materials. Many editors coordinate the activities of all the people involved in preparing technical communications and manage the document development and production processes.

The need for technical writers grew further with the growth of the computer industry beginning in the 1960s. Originally, many computer companies used computer programmers to write user manuals and other documentation. It was widely assumed that the material was so complex that only those who were involved with creating computer programs would be able to write about them. Although computer programmers had the technical knowledge, many were not able to write clear, easy-to-use manuals. Complaints about the difficulty of understanding manuals were common. By the 1970s, computer companies began to hire technical writers to write computer manuals and documents. Today, this is one of the largest areas in which technical writers are employed.

The need for technical marketing writers also grew as a result of expanding computer technology. Many copywriters who worked for advertising agencies and marketing firms did not have the technical background to be able to describe the features of the technical products that were coming to market. Thus developed the need for writers who could combine the ability to promote products with the ability to communicate technical information.

The nature of technical writers' and technical editors' jobs continues to change with emerging technologies. Today, the ability to store, transmit, and receive information through computers and electronic means is changing the very nature of documents. Traditional books and paper documents are being replaced by floppy disks, CD-ROMs, interactive multimedia documents, and material accessed through the Internet.

THE JOB

Technical writers and editors prepare a wide variety of documents and materials. The most common types of documents they produce are manuals, technical reports, specifications, and proposals. Some technical writers also write scripts for videos and audiovisual presentations and text for multimedia programs. Technical writers and editors prepare manuals that give instructions and detailed information on how to install, assemble, use, service, or repair a product or equipment. They may write and edit manuals as simple as a two-page leaflet that gives instructions on how to assemble a bicycle or as complex as a 500-page document that tells service technicians how to repair machinery, medical equipment, or a climate-control system. One of the most common types of manuals is the computer software manual, which informs users on how to install software on their computers, explains how to use the program, and gives information on different features.

Technical writers and editors also prepare technical reports on a multitude of subjects. These reports include documents that give the results of research and laboratory tests and documents that describe the progress of a project. They also write and edit sales proposals, product specifications, quality standards, journal articles, in-house style manuals, and newsletters.

The work of a technical writer begins when he or she is assigned to prepare a document. The writer meets with members of an account or technical team to learn the requirements for the document, the intended purpose or objectives, and the audience. During the planning stage, the writer learns when the document needs to be completed, approximately how long it should be, whether artwork or illustrations are to be included, who the other team members are, and any other production or printing requirements. A schedule is created that defines the different stages of development and determines when the writer needs to have certain parts of the document ready.

The next step in document development is the research, or information gathering, phase. During this stage, technical writers gather all the available information about the product or subject, read and review it, and determine what other information is needed. They may research the topic by reading technical publications, but in most cases they will need to gather information directly from the people working on the product. Writers meet with and interview people who are sources of information, such as scientists, engineers, software developers, computer programmers, managers, and project managers. They ask questions, listen, and take notes or tape record interviews. They gather any available notes, drawings, or diagrams that may be useful.

After writers gather all the necessary information, they sort it out and organize it. They plan how they are going to present the information and prepare an outline for the document. They may decide how the document will look and prepare the design, format, and layout of the pages. In some cases, this may be done by an editor rather than the writer. If illustrations, diagrams, or photographs are going to be included, either the editor or writer makes arrangements for an illustrator, photographer, or art researcher to produce or obtain them.

Then, the writer starts writing and prepares a rough draft of the document. If the document is very large, a writer may prepare it in segments. Once the rough draft is completed, it is submitted to a designated person or group for technical review. Copies of the draft are distributed to managers, engineers, or other experts who can easily determine if any technical information is inaccurate or missing. These reviewers read the document and suggest changes.

The rough draft is also given to technical editors for review of a variety of factors. The editors check that the material is organized well, that each section flows with the section before and after it, and that the language is appropriate for the intended audience. They also check for correct use of grammar, spelling, and punctuation. They ensure that names of parts or objects are consistent throughout the document and that references are accurate. They also check the labeling of graphs and captions for accuracy. Technical editors use special symbols, called proofreader's marks, to indicate the types of changes needed.

The editor and reviewers return their copies of the document to the technical writer. The writer incorporates the appropriate suggestions and revisions and prepares the final draft. The final draft is once again submitted to a designated reviewer or team of reviewers. In some cases, the technical reviewer may do a quick check to make sure that the requested changes were made. In other cases, the technical reviewer may examine the document in depth to ensure technical accuracy and correctness. A walkthrough, or test of the document, may be done for certain types of documents. For example, a walk-through may be done for a document that explains how to assemble a product. A tester assembles the product by following the instructions given in the document. The tester makes a note of all sections that are unclear or inaccurate, and the document is returned to the writer for any necessary revisions.

For some types of documents, a legal review may also be necessary. For example, a pharmaceutical company that is preparing a training manual to teach its sales representatives about a newly released drug needs to ensure that all materials are in compliance with Food and Drug Administration (FDA) requirements. A member of the legal department who is familiar with these requirements will review the document to make sure that all information in the document conforms to FDA rules.

Once the final draft has been approved, the document is submitted to the technical editor, who makes a comprehensive check of the document. In addition to checking that the language is clear and reads smoothly, the editor ensures that the table of contents matches the different sections or chapters of a document, all illustrations and diagrams are correctly placed, all captions are matched to the correct picture, consistent terminology is used, and correct references are used in the bibliography and text.

The editor returns the document to either the writer or a word processor, who makes any necessary corrections. This copy is then checked by a proofreader. The proofreader compares the final copy against the editor's marked-up copy and makes sure that all changes were made. The document is then prepared for printing. In some cases, the writer is responsible for preparing camera-ready copy or electronic files for printing purposes, and in other cases, a print production coordinator prepares all material to submit to a printer.

Some technical writers specialize in a specific type of material. *Technical marketing writers* create promotional and marketing materials for technological products. They may write the copy for an advertisement for a technical product, such as a computer workstation or software, or they may write press releases about the product. They also write sales literature, product flyers, Web pages, and multimedia presentations.

Other technical writers prepare scripts for videotapes and films about technical subjects. These writers, called *scriptwriters*, need to have an understanding of film and video production techniques.

Some technical writers and editors prepare articles for scientific, medical, computer, or engineering trade journals. (See "Science and Medical Writers"). These articles may report the results of research conducted by doctors, scientists, or engineers or report on technological advances in a particular field. Some technical writers and editors also develop textbooks. They may receive articles written by engineers or scientists and edit and revise them to make them more suitable for the intended audience.

Technical writers and editors may create documents for a variety of media. Electronic media, such as compact discs and online services, are increasingly being used in place of books and paper documents. Technical writers may create materials that are accessed through the Internet or create computer-based resources, such as help menus on computer programs. They also create interactive, multimedia documents that are distributed on compact discs or floppy disks. Some of these media require knowledge of special computer programs that allow material to be hyperlinked, or electronically cross-referenced.

REQUIREMENTS

High School

In high school, you should take composition, grammar, literature, creative writing, journalism, social studies, math, statistics, engineering, computer science, and as many science classes as possible. Business courses are also useful as they explain the organizational structure of companies and how they operate.

Postsecondary Training

Most employers prefer to hire technical writers and editors who have a bachelor's or advanced degree. Many technical editors graduate with degrees in the humanities, especially English or journalism. Technical writers typically need to have a strong foundation in engineering, computers, or science. Many technical writers graduate with a degree in engineering or science and take classes in technical writing.

Many different types of college programs are available that prepare people to become technical writers and editors. A growing number of colleges are offering degrees in technical writing. Schools without a technical writing program may offer degrees in journalism or English. Programs are offered through English, communications, and journalism departments. Classes vary based on the type of program. In general, classes for technical writers include a core curriculum in writing and classes in algebra, statistics, logic, science, engineering, and computer programming languages. Useful classes for editors include technical writing, project management, grammar, proofreading, copyediting, and print production.

Many technical writers and editors earn a master's degree. In these programs, they study technical writing in depth and may specialize in a certain area, such as scriptwriting, instructional design, or multimedia applications. In addition, many nondegree writing programs are offered to technical writers and editors to hone their skills. Offered as extension courses or continuing education courses, these programs include courses on indexing, editing medical materials, writing for trade journals, and other related subjects.

Technical writers, and occasionally technical editors, are often asked to present samples of their work. College students should build a portfolio during their college years in which they collect their best samples from work that they may have done for a literary magazine, newsletter, or yearbook.

Technical writers and editors should be willing to pursue learning throughout their careers. As technology changes, technical writers and editors may need to take classes to update their knowledge. Changes in electronic printing and computer technology will also change the way technical writers and editors do their jobs, and writers and editors may need to take courses to learn new skills or new technologies.

Other Requirements

Technical writers need to have good communications skills, science and technical aptitudes, and the ability to think analytically. Technical editors also need to have good communications skills, and judgment, as well as the ability to identify and correct errors in written material. They need to be diplomatic, assertive, and able to explain tactfully what needs to be corrected to writers, engineers, and other people involved with a document. Technical editors should be able to understand technical information easily, but they need less scientific and technical background than writers. Both technical writers and editors need to be able to work as part of a team and collaborate with others on a project. They need to be highly self-motivated, well organized, and able to work under pressure.

EXPLORING

If you enjoy writing and are considering a career in technical writing or editing, you should make writing a daily activity. Writing is a skill that develops over time and through practice. You can keep journals, join writing clubs, and practice different types of writing, such as scriptwriting and informative reports. Sharing writing with others and asking them to critique it is especially helpful. Comments from readers on what they enjoyed about a piece of writing or difficulty they had in understanding certain sections provides valuable feedback that helps to improve your writing style.

Reading a variety of materials is also helpful. Reading exposes you to both good and bad writing styles and techniques, and helps you to identify why one approach works better than another.

You may also gain experience by working on a literary magazine, student newspaper, or yearbook (or starting one of your own if one is not available). Both writing and editing articles and managing production gives you the opportunity to learn new skills and to see what is involved in preparing documents and other materials.

Students may also be able to get internships, cooperative education assignments, or summer or part-time jobs as proofreaders or editorial assistants that may include writing responsibilities.

The Field of Technical Communication

According to the Society for Technical Communication, its 18,000 members include: technical writers and editors, content developers, documentation specialists, technical illustrators, instructional designers, academics, information architects, usability and human factors professionals, visual designers, Web designers and developers, and translators. All of these professionals are required to publish technical information.

EMPLOYERS

There are approximately 50,000 technical writers currently employed in the United States. Editors of all types (including technical editors) hold 127,000 jobs.

Employment may be found in many different types of places, such as in the fields of aerospace, computers, engineering, pharmaceuticals, and research and development, or with the nuclear industry, medical publishers, government agencies or contractors, and colleges and universities. The aerospace, engineering, medical, and computer industries hire significant numbers of technical writers and editors. The federal government, particularly the Departments of Defense and Agriculture, the National Aeronautics and Space Administration (NASA), and the Atomic Energy Commission, also hires many writers and editors with technical knowledge.

STARTING OUT

Many technical writers start their careers as scientists, engineers, technicians, or research assistants and move into writing after several years of experience in those positions. Technical writers with a bachelor's degree in a technical subject such as engineering may be able to find work as a technical writer immediately upon graduating from college, but many employers prefer to hire writers with some work experience.

Technical editors who graduate with a bachelor's degree in English or journalism may find entry-level work as editorial assistants, copy editors, or proofreaders. From these positions they are able to move into technical editing positions. Or beginning workers may find jobs as technical editors in small companies or those with a small technical communications department.

If you plan to work for the federal government, you need to pass an examination. Information about examinations and job openings is available at federal employment centers.

You may learn about job openings through your college's job placement services and want ads in newspapers and professional magazines. You may also research companies that hire technical writers and editors and apply directly to them. Many libraries provide useful job resource guides and directories that provide information about companies that hire in specific areas.

ADVANCEMENT

As technical writers and editors gain experience, they move into more challenging and responsible positions. At first, they may work on simple documents or are assigned to work on sections of a document. As they demonstrate their proficiency and skills, they are given more complex assignments and are responsible for more activities.

Technical writers and editors with several years of experience may move into project management positions. As project managers, they are responsible for the entire document development and production processes. They schedule and budget resources and assign writers, editors, illustrators, and other workers to a project. They monitor the schedule, supervise workers, and ensure that costs remain in budget.

Technical writers and editors who show good project management skills, leadership abilities, and good interpersonal skills may become supervisors or managers. Both technical writers and editors can move into senior writer and senior editor positions. These positions involve increased responsibilities and may include supervising other workers.

Many technical writers and editors seek to develop and perfect their skills rather than move into management or supervisory positions. As they gain a reputation for their quality of work, they may be able to select choice assignments. They may learn new skills as a means of being able to work in new areas. For example, a technical writer may learn a new desktop program in order to become more proficient in designing. Or, a technical writer may learn a hypermedia or hypertext computer program in order to be able to create a multimedia program. Technical writers and editors who broaden their skill base and capabilities can move to higher-paying positions within their own company or at another company. They also may work as freelancers or set up their own communications companies.

EARNINGS

Median annual earnings for salaried technical writers were $55,160 in 2005, according to the Bureau of Labor Statistics. Salaries ranged from less than $33,250 to more than $87,550. Editors of all types earned a median salary of $45,510. The lowest-paid 10 percent earned $26,910 or less and the highest-paid 10 percent earned $85,230 or more. According to a 2005 salary survey conducted by the Society for Technical Communication, the average salary for technical writers and editors is $67,520. The Society for Technical Communication also reports that the median salary of mid-level nonsupervisory technical writers was $53,490 in 2004. The entry-level salary was reported to be $42,500, with senior-level nonsupervisory technical writers earning $66,000.

Most companies offer benefits that include paid holidays and vacations, medical insurance, and 401(k) plans. They may also offer profit sharing, pension plans, and tuition assistance programs.

WORK ENVIRONMENT

Technical writers and editors usually work in an office environment, with well-lit and quiet surroundings. They may have their own offices or share work space with other writers and editors. Most writers and editors have computers. They may be able to utilize the services of support staff who can word process revisions, run off copies, fax material, and perform other administrative functions or they may have to perform all of these tasks themselves.

Some technical writers and editors work out of home offices and use computer modems and networks to send and receive materials electronically. They may go into the office only on occasion for meetings and gathering information. Freelancers and contract workers may work at a company's premises or at home.

Although the standard workweek is 40 hours, many technical writers and editors frequently work 50 or 60 hours a week. Job interruptions, meetings, and conferences can prevent writers from having long periods of time to write. Therefore, many writers work after hours or bring work home. Both writers and editors frequently work in the evening or on weekends in order to meet a deadline.

In many companies there is pressure to produce documents as quickly as possible. Both technical writers and editors may feel at times that they are compromising the quality of their work due to the need to conform to time and budget constraints. In some companies, technical writers and editors may have increased workloads due to company reorganizations or downsizing. They may need to do the work that was formerly done by more than one person. Technical writers and editors also are increasingly assuming roles and responsibilities formerly performed by other people and this can increase work pressures and stress.

Despite these pressures, most technical writers and editors gain immense satisfaction from their work and the roles that they perform in producing technical communications.

OUTLOOK

The writing and editing field is generally very competitive. Each year, there are more people trying to enter this field than there are available openings. The field of technical writing and editing, though, offers more opportunities than other areas of writing and editing, such as book publishing or journalism. Employment opportunities for technical writers and editors are expected to grow about as fast as the average through 2014. Demand is growing for technical writers who can produce well-written computer manuals. In addition to the computer industry, the pharmaceutical industry is showing an increased need for technical writers. Rapid growth in the high technology and electronics industries and the Internet will create a continuing demand for people to write users' guides, instruction manuals, and training materials. Technical writers will be needed to produce copy that describes developments and discoveries in law, science, and technology for a more general audience.

Writers may find positions that include duties in addition to writing. A growing trend is for companies to use writers to run a department, supervise other writers, and manage freelance writers and outside contractors. In addition, many writers are acquiring responsibilities that include desktop publishing and print production coordination.

The demand for technical writers and editors is significantly affected by the economy. During recessionary times, technical writers and editors are often among the first to be laid off. Many companies today are continuing to downsize or reduce their number of employees and are reluctant to keep writers on staff. Such companies prefer to hire writers and editors on a temporary contractual basis, using them only as long as it takes to complete an assigned document. Technical writers and editors who work on a temporary or freelance basis need to market their services and continually look for new assignments. They also do not have the security or benefits offered by full-time employment.

FOR MORE INFORMATION

For information on writing and editing careers in the field of communications, contact
National Association of Science Writers
PO Box 890

Hedgesville, WV 25427-0890
Tel: 304-754-5077
http://www.nasw.org

For information on careers, contact
Society for Technical Communication
901 North Stuart Street, Suite 904
Arlington, VA 22203-1822
Tel: 703-522-4114
Email: stc@stc.org
http://www.stc.org

Writers

QUICK FACTS

School Subjects
English
Journalism

Personal Skills
Communication/ideas
Helping/teaching

Work Environment
Primarily indoors
Primarily one location

Minimum Education Level
Bachelor's degree

Salary Range
$24,320 to $46,420 to
$89,940+

Certification or Licensing
None available

Outlook
About as fast as the average

DOT
131

GOE
01.02.01

NOC
5121

O*NET-SOC
27-3042.00, 27-3043.01,
27-3043.02, 27-3043.03,
27-3043.04

OVERVIEW

Writers express, edit, promote, and interpret ideas and facts in written form for books, magazines, trade journals, newspapers, technical studies and reports, company newsletters, radio and television broadcasts, and advertisements.

Writers develop fiction and nonfiction ideas for plays, novels, poems, and other related works; report, analyze, and interpret facts, events, and personalities; review art, music, film, drama, and other artistic presentations; and persuade the general public to choose or favor certain goods, services, and personalities. There are approximately 192,000 salaried writers, authors, and technical writers employed in the United States.

HISTORY

The skill of writing has existed for thousands of years. Papyrus fragments with writing by ancient Egyptians date from about 3000 B.C., and archaeological findings show that the Chinese had developed books by about 1300 B.C. A number of technical obstacles had to be overcome before printing and the profession of writing evolved. Books of the Middle Ages were copied by hand on parchment. The ornate style that marked these books helped ensure their rarity. Also, few people were able to read.

The development of the printing press by Johannes Gutenberg in the mid-15th century encouraged a wide range of publications, greater literacy, and prompted the development of the publishing industry. The first authors worked directly with printers.

J.K. Rowling, author of the Harry Potter books, makes a special visit to a book store in Edinburgh, Scotland. *(Reuters/Corbis)*

The modern publishing age began in the 18th century. Printing became mechanized, and the novel, magazine, and newspaper were developed. The first newspaper in the American colonies appeared in the early 18th century, but it was Benjamin Franklin who, as editor and writer, made the *Pennsylvania Gazette* one of the most influential in setting a high standard for his fellow American journalists. Franklin also published the first magazine in the colonies, *The American Magazine*, in 1741.

Advances in the printing trades, photoengraving, retailing, and the availability of capital produced a boom in newspapers and magazines in the 19th century. Further mechanization in the printing field, such as the use of the Linotype machine, high-speed rotary presses, and special color reproduction processes, set the stage for still further growth in the book, newspaper, and magazine industry.

In addition to the print media, the broadcasting industry has contributed to the development of the professional writer. Film, radio, and television are sources of entertainment, information, and education that provide employment for thousands of writers.

THE JOB

Writers work in the field of communications. Specifically, they deal with the written word, whether it is destined for the printed page, broadcast, computer screen, or live theater. The nature of writers' work is as varied as the materials they produce: books, magazines, trade journals, newspapers, technical reports, company newsletters and other publications, advertisements, speeches, scripts for motion picture and stage productions, and scripts for radio and television broadcast. Writers develop ideas and write for all media.

Prose writers for newspapers, magazines, and books share many of the same duties. First they come up with an idea for an article or book from their own interests or are assigned a topic by an editor. The topic is of relevance to the particular publication. (For example, a writer for a magazine on parenting may be assigned an article on car seat safety.) Then writers begin gathering as much information as possible about the subject through library research, interviews, the Internet, observation, and other methods. They keep extensive notes from which they draw material for their project. Once the material has been organized and arranged in logical sequence, writers prepare a written outline. The process of developing a piece of writing is exciting, although it can also involve detailed and solitary work. After researching an idea, a writer might discover that a different perspective or related topic would be more effective, entertaining, or marketable.

When working on assignment, writers submit their outlines to an editor or other company representative for approval. Then they write a first draft of the manuscript, trying to put the material into words that will have the desired effect on their audience. They often rewrite or polish sections of the material as they proceed, always searching for just the right way of imparting information or expressing an idea or opinion. A manuscript may be reviewed, corrected, and revised numerous times before a final copy is submitted. Even after that, an editor may request additional changes.

Writers for newspapers, magazines, or books often specialize in their subject matter. Some writers might have an educational background that allows them to give critical interpretations or analyses. For example, a *health* or *science writer* for a newspaper typically has a degree in biology and can interpret new ideas in the field for the average reader.

Columnists or *commentators* analyze news and social issues. They write about events from the standpoint of their own experience or opinion. *Critics* review literary, musical, or artistic works and performances. *Editorial writers* write on topics of public interest, and their comments, consistent with the viewpoints and policies of their employers, are intended to stimulate or mold public opinion. *Newswriters* work for newspapers, radio, or TV news departments, writing news stories from notes supplied by reporters or wire services.

Corporate writers and writers for nonprofit organizations have a wide variety of responsibilities. These writers may work in such places as a large insurance corporation or for a small nonprofit religious group, where they may be required to write news releases, annual reports, speeches for the company head, or public relations materials. Typically they are assigned a topic with length requirements for a given project. They may receive raw research materials, such as statistics, and they are expected to conduct additional research, including personal interviews. These writers must be able to write quickly and accurately on short deadlines, while also working with people whose primary job is not in the communications field. The written work is submitted to a supervisor and often a legal department for approval; rewrites are a normal part of this job.

Copywriters write copy that is primarily designed to sell goods and services. Their work appears as advertisements in newspapers, magazines, and other publications or as commercials on radio and television broadcasts. Sales and marketing representatives first provide information on the product and help determine the style and length of the copy. The copywriters conduct additional research and interviews; to formulate an effective approach, they study advertising trends and review surveys of consumer preferences. Armed with this information, copywriters write a draft that is submitted to the account executive and the client for approval. The copy is often returned for correction and revision until everyone involved is satisfied. Copywriters, like corporate writers, may also write articles, bulletins, news releases, sales letters, speeches, and other related informative and promotional material. Many copywriters are employed in advertising agencies. They also may work for public relations firms or in communications departments of large companies.

Technical writers can be divided into two main groups: those who convert technical information into material for the general public, and those who convey technical information between professionals. Technical writers in the first group may prepare service manuals or handbooks, instruction or repair booklets, or sales literature or brochures; those in the second group may write grant proposals, research reports, contract specifications, or research abstracts (See "Technical Writers and Editors").

Screenwriters prepare scripts for motion pictures or television. They select or are assigned a subject, conduct research, write and submit a plot outline and narrative synopsis (treatment), and confer with the producer and/or director about possible revisions. Screenwriters may adapt books or plays for film and television dramatizations. They often collaborate with other screenwriters and may specialize in a particular type of script or writing.

Playwrights do similar writing for the stage. They write dialogue and describe action for plays that may be tragedies, comedies, or dramas, with themes sometimes adapted from fictional, historical, or narrative sources. Playwrights combine the elements of action, conflict, purpose, and resolution to depict events from real or imaginary life. They often make revisions even while the play is in rehearsal.

Continuity writers prepare the material read by radio and television announcers to introduce or connect various parts of their programs.

Novelists and *short story writers* create stories that may be published in books, magazines, or literary journals. They take incidents from their own lives, from news events, or from their imaginations and create characters, settings, actions, and resolutions. *Poets* create narrative, dramatic, or lyric poetry for books, magazines, or other publications, as well as for special events such as commemorations.

These writers may work with literary agents or editors who help guide them through the writing process, which includes research of the subject matter and an understanding of the intended audience. Many universities and colleges offer graduate degrees in creative writing. In these programs, students work intensively with published writers to learn the art of storytelling.

Writers can be employed either as in-house staff or as freelancers. Pay varies according to experience and the position, but freelancers must provide their own office space and equipment such as computers and fax machines. Freelancers also are responsible for keeping tax records, sending out invoices, negotiating contracts, and providing their own health insurance.

REQUIREMENTS

High School
While in high school, build a broad educational foundation by taking courses in English, literature, foreign languages, history, general science, social studies, computer science, and typing. The ability to type is almost a requisite for all positions in the communications field, as is familiarity with computers.

Postsecondary Training
Competitive writing jobs almost always demand the background of a college education. Many employers prefer you have a broad liberal arts background or majors in English, literature, history, philosophy, or one of the social sciences. Other employers desire communications or journalism training in college. Occasionally a master's degree in a specialized writing field may be required. A number of schools offer courses in journalism, and some of them offer courses or majors in book publishing, publication management, and newspaper and magazine writing.

In addition to formal course work, most employers look for practical writing experience. If you have served on high school or college newspapers, yearbooks, or literary magazines, or if you have worked for small community newspapers or radio stations, even in an unpaid position, you will be an attractive candidate. Many book publishers, magazines, newspapers, and radio and television stations have summer internship programs that provide valuable training if you want to learn about the publishing and broadcasting businesses. Interns do many simple tasks, such as running errands and answering phones, but some may be asked to perform research, conduct interviews, or even write some minor pieces.

Writers who specialize in technical fields may need degrees, concentrated course work, or experience in specific subject areas. This applies frequently to engineering, business, or one of the sciences. Also, technical communications is a degree now offered at many universities and colleges.

If you wish to enter positions with the federal government, you will have to take a civil service examination and meet certain specified requirements, according to the type and level of position.

Other Requirements

To be a writer, you should be creative and able to express ideas clearly, have a broad general knowledge, be skilled in research techniques, and be computer literate. Other assets include curiosity, persistence, initiative, resourcefulness, and an accurate memory. For some jobs—on a newspaper, for example, where the activity is hectic and deadlines are short—the ability to concentrate and produce under pressure is essential.

EXPLORING

As a high school or college student, you can test your interest and aptitude in the field of writing by serving as a reporter or writer

Profile: W. H. Auden (1907–73)

Wystan Hugh Auden is considered one of the most influential 20th-century poets. As the leader of a group of Marxist authors in the 1930s that included Christopher Isherwood and Stephen Spender, Auden wrote many poems brilliantly satirizing middle-class values and attacking Nazism and Fascism. His main concern, however, was with the individual—especially the artist—and his early writings include such simple and moving lyrics as "In Memory of W. B. Yeats" and "Lullaby." His later poetry shows a break with Marxist ideology and an increasing interest in religion and philosophy.

Auden's long poem *The Age of Anxiety* (1947, Pulitzer Prize 1948), about four people in a bar examining life, loneliness, and hope, was also performed on stage. The title became a catchword for the postwar era. In 1956, Auden was given the National Book Award for *The Shield of Achilles*. He received the National Medal for Literature in 1967. In addition to lyric and narrative poems, he wrote verse plays, essays, and librettos. He edited a number of poetry collections.

on school newspapers, yearbooks, and literary magazines. Various writing courses and workshops will provide the opportunity to sharpen your writing skills.

Small community newspapers and local radio stations often welcome contributions from outside sources, although they may not have the resources to pay for them. Jobs in bookstores, magazine shops, and even newsstands will offer you a chance to become familiar with various publications.

You can also obtain information on writing as a career by visiting local newspapers, publishers, or radio and television stations and interviewing some of the writers who work there. Career conferences and other guidance programs frequently include speakers on the entire field of communications from local or national organizations.

EMPLOYERS

There are approximately 142,000 writers and authors and 50,000 technical writers currently employed in the United States. Nearly half of salaried writers and editors work in the information sector, which includes newspapers, magazines, book publishers, radio and television broadcasting, software publishers, and Internet businesses. Writers also work for advertising agencies and public relations firms and work on journals and newsletters published by business and nonprofit organizations, such as professional associations, labor unions, and religious organizations. Other employers are government agencies and film production companies.

STARTING OUT

A fair amount of experience is required to gain a high-level position in the field. Most writers start out in entry-level positions. These jobs may be listed with college placement offices, or they may be obtained by applying directly to the employment departments of the individual publishers or broadcasting companies. Graduates who previously served internships with these companies often have the advantage of knowing someone who can give them a personal recommendation. Want ads in newspapers and trade journals are another source for jobs. Because of the competition for positions, however, few vacancies are listed with public or private employment agencies.

Employers in the communications field usually are interested in samples of published writing. These are often assembled in an organized portfolio or scrapbook. Bylined or signed articles are more credible (and, as a result, more useful) than stories whose source is not identified.

Entry-level positions as a junior writer usually involve library research, preparation of rough drafts for part or all of a report, cataloging, and other related writing tasks. These are generally carried on under the supervision of a senior writer.

Some technical writers have entered the field after working in public relations departments or as technicians or research assistants, then transferring to technical writing as openings occur. Many firms now hire writers directly upon recommendation of college professors and placement offices.

ADVANCEMENT

Most writers find their first jobs as editorial or production assistants. Advancement may be more rapid in small companies, where beginners learn by doing a little bit of everything and may be given writing tasks immediately. In large firms, duties are usually more compartmentalized. Assistants in entry-level positions are assigned such tasks as research, fact-checking, and copyrighting, but it generally takes much longer to advance to full-scale writing duties.

Promotion into more responsible positions may come with the assignment of more important articles and stories to write, or it may be the result of moving to another company. Mobility among employees in this field is common. An assistant in one publishing house may switch to an executive position in another. Or a writer may switch to a related field as a type of advancement.

A technical writer can be promoted to positions of responsibility by moving from such jobs as writer to technical editor to project leader or documentation manager. Opportunities in specialized positions also are possible.

Freelance or self-employed writers earn advancement in the form of larger fees as they gain exposure and establish their reputations.

EARNINGS

In 2005, median annual earnings for salaried writers and authors were $46,420 a year, according to the Bureau of Labor Statistics. The lowest-paid 10 percent earned less than $24,320, while the highest-paid 10 percent earned $89,940 or more. In book publishing, some specialties pay better than others. Technical writers earned a median salary of $55,160 in 2005, with entry-level salaries averaging around $42,500 a year.

In addition to their salaries, many writers earn some income from freelance work. Part-time freelancers may earn from $5,000 to

$15,000 a year. Freelance earnings vary widely. Full-time established freelance writers may earn up to $75,000 a year.

WORK ENVIRONMENT

Working conditions vary for writers. Although their workweek usually runs 35 to 40 hours, many writers work overtime. A publication that is issued frequently has more deadlines closer together, creating greater pressures to meet them. The work is especially hectic on newspapers and at broadcasting companies, which operate seven days a week. Writers often work nights and weekends to meet deadlines or to cover a late-developing story.

Most writers work independently, but they often must cooperate with artists, photographers, rewriters, and advertising people who may have widely differing ideas of how the materials should be prepared and presented.

Physical surroundings range from comfortable private offices to noisy, crowded newsrooms filled with other workers typing and talking on the telephone. Some writers must confine their research to the library or telephone interviews, but others may travel to other cities or countries or to local sites, such as theaters, ballparks, airports, factories, or other offices.

The work is arduous, but most writers are seldom bored. Some jobs, such as that of the foreign correspondent, require travel. The most difficult element is the continual pressure of deadlines. People who are the most content as writers enjoy and work well with deadline pressure.

OUTLOOK

The employment of writers is expected to increase at an average rate through 2014, according to the U.S. Department of Labor. Competition for writing jobs has been and will continue to be competitive. The demand for writers by newspapers, periodicals, book publishers, and nonprofit organizations is expected to increase. The growth of online publishing on company Web sites and other online services will also create a demand for many talented writers; those with computer skills will be at an advantage as a result. The fields of advertising and public relations should also provide job opportunities.

The major book and magazine publishers, broadcasting companies, advertising agencies, public relations firms, and the federal government account for the concentration of writers in large cities such as New York, Chicago, Los Angeles, Boston, Philadelphia,

San Francisco, and Washington, D.C. Opportunities with small newspapers, corporations, and professional, religious, business, technical, and trade publications can be found throughout the country.

People entering this field should realize that the competition for jobs is extremely keen. Beginners may have difficulty finding employment. Of the thousands who graduate each year with degrees in English, journalism, communications, and the liberal arts, intending to establish a career as a writer, many turn to other occupations when they find that applicants far outnumber the job openings available. College students would do well to keep this in mind and prepare for an unrelated alternate career in the event they are unable to obtain a position as writer; another benefit of this approach is that they can become qualified as writers in a specialized field. The practicality of preparing for alternate careers is borne out by the fact that opportunities are best in firms that prepare business and trade publications and in technical writing. Job candidates with good writing skills and knowledge of a specialized area such as economics, finance, computer programming, or science will have the best chances of finding jobs.

Potential writers who end up working in a different field may be able to earn some income as freelancers, selling articles, stories, books, and possibly TV and movie scripts, but it is usually difficult for writers to support themselves entirely as independent writers.

FOR MORE INFORMATION

For information on writing and editing careers in the field of communications, contact

National Association of Science Writers
PO Box 890
Hedgesville, WV 25427-0890
Tel: 304-754-5077
http://www.nasw.org

This organization offers student memberships for those interested in opinion writing.

National Conference of Editorial Writers
3899 North Front Street
Harrisburg, PA 17110-1583
Tel: 717-703-3015
Email: ncew@pa-news.org
http://www.ncew.org

For information on scholarships and student memberships aimed at those preparing for a career in technical communication, contact
Society for Technical Communication
901 North Stuart Street, Suite 904
Arlington, VA 22203-1822
Tel: 703-522-4114
Email: stc@stc.org
http://www.stc.org

Index

Entries and page numbers in bold indicate major treatment of a topic.